Restauranting 101:
The Eight Basic Fundamentals

Build the restaurant of your dreams in the next 90 days.

My goal is to start a revolution, I want every restaurant owner in America to *get positive* and *think bigger*. I want every restaurant owner to focus on the reasons why we can do it, instead of why we cannot.

My goal is the teach restaurant owners and managers like you, to focus on Eight Basic Fundamentals which lead to:

1. Happy customers who spread the good word about your restaurant.
2. A team of full-time winners who work harder than you do to achieve the mission.
3. Increased sales, financial freedom, and a better life.

You can do it... I'll show you how.

Chef Peter Harman, The Food Guru

Contact the Author: foodguru@foodguru.com

Table of Contents

Introduction

This is the greatest time in the history of the world to be alive, and the future is going to be even better. It's time stop fooling around and start kicking ass.

It doesn't matter where you started, what happened yesterday, or what happened ten years ago. You do not live in the past, you cannot change the past, the past is gone. You live in the present. Today is all there is. The only thing that matters is what you do today. Are you going to dig deep holes to hide in, or are you going to build big glorious castles in the sky and share them with the world?

You are an amazing human being. You have come to this planet at this time to create abundance for your family, friends, staff, and community. You are here to thrive. In fact, your *job* is to thrive! The world wants, and *needs*, you to thrive so you can become rich, bless your family, your employees, and the people around you. Don't let them down!

- Little people do little things.
- Average people do average things.
- Great people do *great* things.

A Restaurant Story

Let's begin our journey with a short story about restaurants:

- 80% of restaurants live between Failure & Survival
- 14% of restaurants live between Survival & Success
- The Top 5% of restaurants Succeed
- The Top 1% of restaurants Thrive

80% of Restaurants Live Between Failure & Survival

80% of all restaurant owners are slaves to their business. They work for the bank, the investors, the landlord, the vendors, the customers, and their employees. Most restaurant owners struggle to pay their bills, they live by robbing Peter to pay Paul. One wrong move can put most of all restaurants out of business for good!

80% of independent restaurant owners and managers are not professional business people. They are simply passengers along for the ride, toiling away in their area of technical expertise, cooking, bartending, marketing, or accounting. Most restaurant owners and managers lack the skills and mindset required to win.

80% of restaurant owners and managers believe it is impossible to find good, quality people when they need them. They hire warm bodies who care more about days off, tips, smoke breaks, and staying connected on Facebook than they do about learning the restaurant craft, improving their performance, and delivering a great customer experience.

80% of all restaurants have no system or consistent way to do things. The important decisions are made on a daily basis by under-trained, self-entitled, part-time employees—not qualified leaders.

The level of customer service comes down to who is at work today, and what mood they're in. The hourly employees determine when (or, *if*) they are going to show up, how much work they will do, and what the service standards of the restaurant will be, today. The animals are running the zoo!

Attendance standards in most restaurants are a joke! Most managers cannot write an effective schedule to save their lives. Staff turnover is out of control. There are no training standards or checklists for employees and managers to follow. Very few restaurants have written standards for purchasing, receiving, inventory, production, marketing, or basic plate presentation.

80% of all restaurant owners do not have a mission, a goal, a clear vision of their concept, or systems to manage the business. Most restaurant owners have the wrong mindset going into the venture. They compete for "market share" by chasing the latest restaurant fad, they simply follow the herd. They use coupons, deals, and discounts as their secret marketing weapons, fighting to win "the race to the bottom".

The people who own and manage these restaurants can rarely afford to take a day off, and when they do, they are usually too exhausted, and too broke to have fun. This is reality for 80% of all restaurants. Does this sound familiar?

14% of Restaurants Live Between Survival & Success

14% of restaurants live between basic survival and success. 14% of restaurants owners have a well-defined concept and a basic operating system. These people know how to run a restaurant and make a small profit. However; these restaurants tend to be inconsistent; they are great in some areas and weak in others.

The key element of their success is the presence of the owner or a strong key manager. The place runs great when they are there, but it falls apart the minute the owner or manager walk out the door. There has to be a better way.

5% of Restaurants Succeed

The Top 5% of restaurants succeed. That's right. Only 5% of all restaurants in America are well-run systems-dependent businesses. Only 5% of all restaurants have good consistent leadership and perform correctly when the owner is not present. These restaurants have a simple concept, simple business plan, good training system, people who accept responsibility and do their jobs 100%.

The managers and staff are usually on time, in the proper uniform, and at their station working when they are scheduled. These restaurants create opportunity for growth and advancement, if you work hard, stay focused and exemplify the restaurant culture.

The kitchen, bar, dining room and bathrooms are clean, the paint on the walls is fresh. The tv, the music and the ambiance compliment the theme of the restaurant. The sales and costs are usually in line with the budget. These restaurants do most things the right way and the owner is earning a 10% profit, the gold standard in our industry.

1% of Restaurants Thrive

The Top 1% of restaurants Thrive. The Top 1% create a culture of excellence from the owner to the newest cook. These restaurants have a clear mission and core values that are "etched in stone". The staff knows and understands what the expectations are, and they work their asses off to meet and exceed those goals and standards.

The main difference between the restaurants that Succeed (Top 5%) and the ones that Thrive (Top 1%) is the quality of the people and their level of commitment. The Top 1% have *full-time*, quality people in every position. The staff are well-paid, professionals who love what they do for a living.

The restaurants that reach the Thrive Level have built a culture of excellence. They have a solid core of professional managers, chefs, cooks, bartenders, and service people who constantly seek ways to improve their products and performance. The people who work in these places are world-class artisans with a high degree of knowledge, talent, character and integrity.

Why does one restaurant Thrive and another Fail?

The restaurants that thrive, focus on the basic fundamentals of the restaurant business and frequently ask, "How can we do this better?"

The Thrive Level is not a utopia. The thrive level is what your restaurant could and should be. Restaurants that Thrive create a culture of excellence. They believe there is a better way to do everything, and they work hard every day to achieve it. Restaurants that Thrive, focus on improvement and innovation, they constantly move the ball forward.

Building a great restaurant does not require being in a certain city or state with a large population, because if that were true, all the best restaurants would be in the same large city. Building a great restaurant does not require a fancy degree or social pedigree, if that were true, all the great restaurants would be owned by people from places like Cornell University or the Culinary Institute of America (CIA).

Age doesn't matter, because if that were true, all the great restaurateurs would be the same age. The same can be said for ethnic background, skin color, and religion.

The truth is, great restaurants can be found anywhere from a taco truck in San Antonio to a five-star dining room in Las Vegas. Great restaurants have been started by people of all ages. Did you know that Ray Kroc didn't open his first McDonald's until the ripe old age 54? The best restaurants are owned and managed by a wide range of people, from a wide variety of backgrounds.

Here's a list of why most restaurants fail:

- No clear purpose, goal, or mission
- Lack of leadership and bad management
- No consistency or conformity
- Trying to please all the people all the time
- Failure to improve, innovate and adapt
- Terrible location
- Stupid concept or weird food
- Major catastrophe or legal problems
- Alcohol or drug abuse
- Moral corruption
- Part-time employee attitude
- "Entitlement Syndrome"

4

The Eight Basic Fundamentals

In all my years of experience and study in the restaurant business, I have found that there are Eight Basic Fundamentals that make the difference between winning and losing, and that's what this book is all about. Times change, fashions change, tools change, but these eight basic fundamentals *never* change.

These are the basic fundamentals of the restaurant business. These fundamentals are mandatory in every type of restaurant. These are not "get rich quick" schemes, these are the basic universal truths and fundamentals that will work in every restaurant, every time, in every city around the world.

In this book, we will focus on Eight Basic Fundamentals. As you will see, these basic fundamentals are simple and very easy to do AND these basic fundamentals are also very easy to blow off and not do.

Most restaurant owners and managers are buried, trying to do 1,000 different things at the same time. Starting today, you are going to stop the madness, and focus on Eight Basic Fundamentals!

I Repeat: Starting today you are going to focus on Eight Basic Fundamentals. These eight fundamentals will transform your restaurant from *OK* to *GREAT* in the next 90 days. (*Did he just say 90-days?*) Yes, I did!

The Eight Basic Fundamentals are:

1. Set & Achieve a Noble Goal
2. Develop the Owner Mindset
3. Build a Winning Team
4. Build a Customer-Centered Brand
5. Build a Better Marketing & Sales System
6. Build a Better Money Management System
7. Build a Bullet-Proof Operating System
8. Improve, Innovate & Adapt

Fundamental #1:
Set & Achieve a Noble Goal

This is about getting you headed in the right direction. I have found that most people (80%) have no clear goals, dreams or plan for their lives.

Most people spend their days reacting to external stimulus, the people, events, and situations around them. The average person wanders around, and life just sort of "happens" to them. It is the same for restaurant owners, they chase the latest fads trying to stay relevant and run from one problem to the next, trying to do 1,000 different things. Simplicity, repetition and consistency are the key to success in our business.

People with clear goals succeed, while people with vague, ambiguous goals, flounder. Building a great restaurant requires a clear goal and a simple plan to get there.

Fundamental #2:
Develop the Owner Mindset

You are the sum-total of every thought you have ever had. Your actions have created the life you have today, your decisions have put you exactly where you are today. If you are not happy with your life or the performance of your restaurant, then something needs to change, and that change begins with you. This is the best time in history to be in the restaurant business and the future will be even better.

The truth is, if you are struggling today, it's your own damn fault. It's time to be honest with yourself and face the truth: You are the one who is writing the script for your restaurant and your life. It's time to stop blaming other people for your personal situation. It's time to face the truth and accept responsibility. It's time to stop making excuses and start making adjustments that will move the ball forward to victory.

Fundamental #3:
Build a Winning Team

You will only be as successful as your people want you to be. This fundamental is about being a great recruiter, developing talent, and building a team of full-time winners who work as hard as you do.

Fundamental #4:
Build a Customer-Centered Brand

This fundamental is about creating a brand that your customers will love, support, and rally behind. This is about determining the exact experience you want your customers to have from the time they enter the restaurant until they pay the check and leave.

We are in the hospitality business, and the customer is the real reason we are here. This fundamental is about writing the script for your restaurant and delivering the customer promise.

Fundamental #5:
Build a Better Marketing & Sales System

I will show you how to effectively use marketing and in-store sales to dramatically increase revenue. The ideas in this book are very simple and straightforward. These ideas WILL work in any type of restaurant! These ideas WILL work for you.

One of my restaurants used this system, and their sales went from $840,000 to $1,050,000 in the first year (a 24% increase). Another restaurant used this system to increase sales by 56% the first year, 40% in the second year, and 20% in the third year. Another client that I started a restaurant for, has just opened their THIRD location.

Hold on tight… your sales are about to explode!

Fundamental #6:
Build a Better Money Management System

The goal here is simple: Sales must be 10% greater than expenses. This fundamental is about re-imagining your money management system and building a thriving business that earns a ten percent profit, year after year, after year. This simple process will make you money—lots of money!

Fundamental #7:
Build a Bullet-Proof Operating System

This fundamental is about giving our people the information (the answers) that tells them how we do it here. We use the system to train our people to run the business in an effective and professional manner, even when you are not there.

The system includes, food and bar recipes with pictures. Checklists and procedures for everything, from sweeping the floor to answering the phone. The strength of your system will determine your level of success. Great systems create wealth while bad systems destroy wealth.

Fundamental #8:
Improve, Innovate & Adapt

This fundamental is the action and improvement fundamental. When you have gone through the steps above, you will start to ask the most important questions:

- How can we do this better?
- How can we add value to the product, the team, the business, the brand and the customer experience?
- How do we create more abundance?

The goal here is to improve by 1% every day. If you take a two week of vacation every year and one day off every week, that leaves 300 days for work each year. When you improve by 1% every day, that adds up to a 300% improvement every year. *This process can literally change your life.*

My Goal for You

My goal is to help you and your restaurant THRIVE! My goal is to help you build the BEST restaurant in your market. We will start the process with a simple and in my opinion VERY achievable goal.

As your new coach, my first challenge for you is to increase the sales in your restaurant by 10% TWICE, in the next 90-Days! Yes, this can and will happen, when you decide to get serious. The truth is that you don't have to believe that this is possible right now. All you have to do is keep reading and allow me to show you WHY this is possible for you.

These Eight Basic Fundamentals will help you cut through the clutter and get to the essence of building a great restaurant. Just imagine what will happen when your entire team works together toward a common goal, and seeks to find intelligent, creative ways to improve every aspect of the business and the customer experience.

Think of a fresh Apple. When we remove the skin and the flesh, we are left with the seeds. The seeds contain the DNA that makes the apple an apple. If any of the seeds are defective in any way, future apples will also be defective. When we improve the seeds (the way we think), our future apples will be bigger, better, juicier and more delicious.

Think of the Eight Basic Fundamentals as the seeds of your restaurant. If your seeds are defective, your restaurant will never reach its potential. My goal is to help you analyze, understand and re-imagine the basic fundamentals, the DNA of your restaurant. When you improve your restaurant DNA, every aspect of your business will improve.

These Eight Basic Fundamentals will help you and your entire team create a culture of excellence and work together toward a common goal.

These Eight Basic Fundamentals will help you find intelligent ways to improve every aspect of your restaurant. Individually these Eight Basic Fundamentals add up to

$1 + 1 + 1 + 1 + 1 + 1 + 1 + 1 =$ an 8x IMPROVEMENT, which is pretty good.

When these Eight Basic Fundamentals are used together as part of a smart system, they can have an amazing compounding effect—your business will take giant leaps forward. This is called EXPONENTIAL growth!

Think of the fundamentals as:

$1 \rightarrow 2 \rightarrow 4 \rightarrow 8 \rightarrow 16 \rightarrow 32 \rightarrow 64 \rightarrow 128x$

The Most Direct Route To The Target

This is a relatively short book because it only focuses on the important stuff. These Eight Basic Fundamentals will help you transform your restaurant from OK to Great in the next 90 days.

This is not a shortcut. This is simply the fastest and most direct route to the target. This information will help you and your business become 128x more effective than you are today!

This book is a collection of common ideas with the potential to have an uncommon effect on your restaurant and your life. These ideas are time-tested fundamentals that work every time, in every type of restaurant.

This Is Not A Sprint... It's A Marathon

If you are the owner, how long do you plan to own your restaurant? If you are a chef, bartender manager, or star of the future, how long do plan to be in this business, or in any business for that matter?

I find that most people have a very short-term mindset. They only focus on this week, this month, this quarter, or this year.

In contrast, the greatest thinkers have a long-term view. Think about Google Maps for a moment. You can zoom in and see your house or your restaurant and/or you can zoom out and see the entire planet. The most successful people have the ability to do both: Big thinkers have the ability to zoom in and zoom out. They see their world from a 360-degree view, the whole thing from the inside and the outside.

Smart operators see their restaurant and their business as it is, and as it could be. Big thinkers have the ability to see beyond what it is today, and they also have the ability to visualize what could tomorrow, if & when they get serious and take charge of their life and their situation.

When I think of you, I see two people. I see the person that you are today, AND I see the person that you have the potential to become. The direction that you choose is completely up to you.

My goal is to help you transform your restaurant and your life. If you are sick of just scraping by, and truly want to improve, the ideas in this little book can help you develop your own recipe for success. These ideas can help both, beginners & successful restaurant veterans. You don't need to know everything; you just need to know (and do) the right things. This book will catapult your knowledge from where ever you are today, into the Top 5% of all restaurant owners.

This book is for:

- Independent restaurant owners who are struggling to stay alive.
- Restaurant managers who are looking for straight answers.
- Stars of the future who want to Win!

Whether you are the owner, the manager, or a star of the future, you must develop the "Restaurant Owner's Mindset" and look at your restaurant from a positive perspective.

"A Dull Pencil Beats A Sharp Mind"

I highly recommend that you keep a pad and pen with you as you read this book. I use the recorder function on my iPhone, because it would be a shame to lose a great idea.

The best ideas will come from inside your brain. I wrote this book to make you *think*! As you read this material, your subconscious mind will either agree or disagree with my points. Whether you agree with me or not, is unimportant. My goal is to challenge your beliefs and make you think!

When you read a point that you disagree with, stop and ask yourself, "Why do I disagree with this point or idea?" Does the idea challenge the status quo and push you outside your comfort zone? If what you are doing today is only creating mediocre results, something big needs to change in order for you to thrive.

My goal is to challenge your thinking, stretch your mind, and help you thrive! This book will create fantastic new ideas in your mind that you can use to improve. This reading, thinking, and a note-taking process can—and will—change your life, if you have the guts and focus to use the ideas that you generate!

Sharing Is Good

As you read this book and learn the fundamentals, it is critical that you share this information with your people. To understand this information is great, but you must share these ideas with your people. This book can be a great tool to get everyone on the same page, speaking the same language. Buy one for all of your key people today.

Against The Grain

I know that restaurant owners are very "independent thinkers", I am sure you will not agree with everything I have to say, and that is fine with me. As you will see, I have a very strong opinion about most things, too. I intend to rattle your cage, piss you off, and make you think!

If you are not 100% satisfied with your situation, that means it's time for something to change, and that change, must start with YOU!

The fact that you are holding this book in your hands proves that you are interested in finding a better way! Let's see if we can find it together.

I Want To Be Your Coach

We all love to read and learn, which is great. The problem is that most people don't do anything with the knowledge. Building a smart plan and taking action is the real key to success! I can help you win!

Change is hard. How many people know that smoking is bad for them, but still continue to smoke? How many people know that exercise is good for them, but still don't exercise?

We all need a coach to help us get over our mental hurdles, stay focused and do the work. Everybody needs someone to talk to who understands their problems. You need a non-judgmental third party who can help you get strategic and develop a system to accomplish your goals and dreams. Most importantly you need a coach to keep you focused on the mission.

Welcome to the World of the Food Guru

My name is Peter Harman. I am the Food Guru. I create, design, build, and fix restaurants. I have spent my entire career, turning broken restaurants into winners. I can help you improve your restaurant and your life. The answers that I am going to share with you are very simple. In fact, all the great truths of life are simple.

The restaurant business is one of the toughest businesses on earth. As a restaurant owner, you must be able to juggle the needs of your family, business partners, customers, employees, managers, time, and money, all at the once.

I know that you rarely have enough time or money to do things the way you really want to do them. The margin of error in our business is small and getting smaller every day. To survive in this business, you must be damn-near perfect at everything. Staying alive is difficult, and the idea of financial freedom often seems like an impossible dream.

I imagine that you are a restaurant owner, manager, or star of the future who is not satisfied with your current circumstances. If you are an owner, I imagine there have been weeks when you have not been able to pay yourself. I know that you pray that your payroll checks don't bounce. I know how you feel. I've been there myself… way too many times. Let me tell you my story.

My Story

I started my career in Florida working as a chef, then executive chef, and food & beverage director at several very large resorts. I considered myself a successful F&B guy. During my Florida career, I had some amazing coaches and mentors who kicked my ass and taught me how to build and manage a professional business.

In 1996, I moved my family to Iowa to start my own company, Menu Innovators. This company ran Martini's Grille, a little Italian restaurant called Moosellini's and a big banquet operation. In 2004, I moved Martini's Grille to our current location high above the Mississippi River.

Then, things really took off. I took a HUGE Bite!

From 2004 – 2008, I opened 8 new restaurants. The new Martini's Grille, Lips To Go, Food Guru University (my cooking school) Chicks of Macomb, Graze Iowa City, Graze Davenport, Graze West Des Moines and the Captain's

11

Table in Moline. People were handing me money—lots of money—to open restaurants.

I also wrote three cookbooks, The Manly Art of Macho Cookery, The Martini's Grille Cookbook and Martini's Martinis. In 2005, I was the first chef to produce a cooking video podcast. I produced over 300 cooking videos for both podcast and television broadcast on NBC affiliates in Iowa and Illinois. At one point, my "Food Guru Moments" video podcast had over one million subscribers. My company was on a roll, life was fun, crazy, hectic, and awesome!

Then in late 2008 and 2009, the big bad recession came, and it kicked my ass!!

I ran right into the biggest recession since 1929 and the Great Depression, I wasn't prepared. At that time, my oldest restaurant (Martini's) was four years old, but my youngest two restaurants were less than six months old. I simply grew too fast. I didn't have the financial stability or right people in the right places, we were not equipped to handle the financial meltdown of the economy. My investors ran for exits. I had to close one of my restaurants (*the worst day of my life*) and pull the license agreement from another. I had a two-year legal battle with another group of partners (*a stupid mis-understanding*) that started when a wealthy doctor's wife erroneously thought her husband's $5,000 investment was a $100,000 investment, what a mess.

My point is, I know what it's like to build the business of your dreams, and then watch it explode. I know what it feels like to get pummeled in the newspaper, on TV, and on Facebook. I know what it feels like to go broke and start over. I know what it feels like to get swallowed by the beast and get shat-out the other end, *and* I have all the battle scars to prove it.

The Wind Beneath My Wings

The greatest asset that I have in my life is my sweet little farm girl wife Kim. She has been with me every step of the way, since we married in 2001.

Kim helped me climb the mountain *and* she was there when we the shit hit the fan in 2009, she was right there as we both went tumbling down the mountain, together, into the valley of darkness.

Imagine the aftermath of a tornado – #@^*!! Time to start again...

Together we, dusted ourselves off, gritted our teeth and put our heads down. Kim has helped me keep my sanity during our journey through the valley and back up the mountain. Together we re-built our company and our lives. Kim is my absolute hero, best friend and business partner.

Today, we are kicking ass and living the lives of our dreams. I have no idea who or where I would be without my little farm girl wife.

Picking Up The Pieces

In 2009, I re-dedicated myself to becoming a smarter leader and building a better business. I started writing the book you now hold in your hands. I started writing just to maintain sanity, clarify my thinking and teach my managers & staff.

Henry Ford once said, "You can take everything away from me and I'll rebuild it smarter and better in five years."

Well, it took me a little longer than that to rebuild, but today, I am alive and well! Our business has morphed into a more mature, thoughtful organization. Today, I run two restaurants, Graze Iowa City and Martini's Grille in Burlington, Iowa. We are in the process of moving Graze to a new amazing location in early-2020.

In addition to the restaurants, my long-term goal is to use my expertise to help people like you build the restaurant of your dreams and thrive in this exciting and crazy world.

It breaks my heart to see someone invest their own money and the money of their friends and families, only to watch it go straight down the drain. It kills me to see smart, hard-working people work their ass off 60-70-80 hours a week and have nothing to show for it. I don't know everything, but I know I can help you get to the next level.

Albert Einstein once said, "The significant problems we face today cannot be solved with the level of thinking that was used to create them." That means the thinking that got you here, will not get you to the next level. You must improve and expand your thinking.

We All Need Help

The truth is, we all get mentally stuck at a certain level, and it's almost impossible to get unstuck, all by ourselves. We all need someone to help us see the reality that is holding us back. We all need a coach, to help us move forward.

I am your new coach. I am going to help you move forward & thrive. I know that you may be living in denial or thinking you can get unstuck all by yourself. I know that you're afraid (at least very uncomfortable) to ask for help. The reality is that if you could have figured it out, and fixed it by yourself, you would have done it by now.

It doesn't matter what level you're at:

- You could be circling the drain about to file bankruptcy
- Or trying to grow from a 7% to a 10% profit.
- Or, double the number of stores you operate.

I know that you don't want to admit that you are stuck and need help… nobody does. It takes courage—real courage—to ask for help. Reading this book is a great place to start.

About This Book

I wrote this book to inspire every single person to do their very best to excel in the restaurant business. This includes every chef, bartender, manager, owner, star of the future and even the CEOs of large restaurant companies.

The process that I am about to share with you will not cost you one penny more than you are already spending today. This process will change your life and make you money—lots of money! The information in this book will work… and it will work every time, in any type of restaurant.

At the end of each chapter, I'm going to ask you to write *TEN* things that you can do to improve each fundamental. At the end of the book, you will have *SEVENTY* great ideas that came straight out of your brain to start this process. Be sure to do this… *don't blow it off!*

If you read this book and implement the ideas, you and your restaurant will thrive. These are not voodoo spells or "get rich quick" schemes, these are universal truths that anyone with a fifth-grade education can understand and follow.

However, these ideas are also very easy to blow off and not follow.

Statistics show that about 5% of the people who read this book, (or any book for that matter) will actually use the information. Sadly, that's only about one out of twenty! This is because, reading is easy, taking action and doing the work, is hard.

It doesn't matter who you are, where you come from, or where you are at today, what matters is your ability to adapt, improve and persevere. If you are new to the restaurant business, this book will open your mind and improve your knowledge quickly. This little book can help you jump start your career and make you more valuable. This book will put you on the path to that big fat paycheck you deserve.

Remember, this is your life. This is not a dress rehearsal.

If you are already an accomplished restaurateur or the CEO of a large restaurant group, I'm sure you will have heard many of these points before, but the big questions are:

1. Are you using the information to improve your business?
2. Do your people have this information?
3. And are they putting it to work?

This book will serve as a highlight reel of basic fundamentals and issues your people are struggling with. This book can be used to help you become a better leader and inspire your people.

You are Only Performing at 40% of Your Potential

This is true of most people in all walks of life. Most people are just going through the motions, reacting to life as it comes. Very few people have a real plan and stick with it no matter what.

The best athletes and most successful people have coaches to help them improve and stay focused on the right things. This book is the tool to help you and your people get and stay focused on the right things. This book can help you, and your organization break through the grunge and clutter. This book can help you thrive.

Most restaurant people are simply busy being busy, trying to do a thousand new and different things, day after day, after day, after day. They spend all their time dealing with minutiae and ten-cent problems that burn them out. Most restaurant owners are too exhausted to see the $1,000,000 opportunities that are all around them every day.

I want to help you switch your focus from "problem obsession" to a "vision of opportunity". The restaurant business isn't as hard as most people make it look. Just imagine what could happen in your restaurant, if you could double your output and performance.

Your New Journey Begins Right Here, Right Now

Start by reading this book from cover to cover. Then take a few days away from the restaurant. You need time to think deeply about your future. The goal is to get out of your cage and see your situation from the outside, the big picture, the long-term view of your life. You do realize that your life is more than just your restaurant, don't you?

In the world of public relations, they have a saying, *"When you are in a hole, stop digging!"* This rule applies to you today: If your restaurant is in a hole, you must stop digging!

If you can't get away right now because your people are out of control and the restaurant can't survive one single day without you, I would seriously recommend that you close the shop for a day or two. I'm serious. You need to get off the treadmill and allow yourself some time to think. You need time away from the daily grind to contemplate your future.

After you take your little journey, you will be ready to hit the "restart" button and begin the exciting process of "Re-Imagining Your Restaurant". Building a great restaurant is a lifelong quest. It doesn't happen overnight, or even on the first attempt. Everyone has different strengths and weaknesses. You are where you are, and your new journey begins right here, right now!

The world is changing fast and we must challenge "conventional wisdom" at every step of the process. Every day of your life you see things that don't work for you, things you wish you could change.

The longing or angst that you feel in the middle of the night is not from the mistakes of your past. The longing or angst that you feel in the middle of the night it is your future greatness calling you to take your rightful seat at the table.

I am giving you the *power* to change anything that you want, and I am giving you *permission* to do (and become) anything you wish. All you have to do is take control of your life and make a few simple changes. This sounds simple and great… because it is.

You can do it! I'll show you how.

I say that all the time to my partners, my employees, and my clients. It may sound like a cliché to you, but the fact is, I say it all the time because I truly believe it. The ideas in this book have worked in the past, they work today, and they *will* work for you, too… *if* you apply them.

Now, let's go start a revolution.

Fundamental #1:
Set & Achieve a Noble Goal

This fundamental is about setting a noble goal. A noble goal is something worthy of your God-given time and talent that will give great benefit to you, your family, your friends and the world around you. A noble goal is the quest for something larger than yourself.

Before we start talking about goals, I want you to understand that this is your actual life. This is not a dress-rehearsal. This is the REAL thing, this is not a game, this is not practice.

Are you living the life of your dreams? Are you happy with where you are today? If you continue on your current path, where will you be in five years? How about 10 years? Will that make you happy?

Is your current path going to deliver you to where you really want to be? If the answer is no, it's time to make some changes. *It's time to Giddy Up!*

What Are Your Goals?

What do you want to be when you grow up? I love asking people that question. It always catches them off guard. It throws them for a loop. But it is the most important question of all, isn't it? I am going to start this chapter by dissecting five quotes.

The first quote is by Earl Nightingale: *"People with goals succeed because they know where they are going."* This is really obvious, but do you know where you are going? Do you really have a well mapped out plan? Or, are you just living day to day, going with the flow?

The second quote is by Ralph Waldo Emerson: *"We become what we think about all day long."* This is simply brilliant. What do you think about all day? Video games, Facebook, or something bad? Are your thoughts positive or negative? Do your thoughts move you toward your goal, or keep you locked in place?

Now the third quote, is by John F. Kennedy: *"Things do not happen, things are made to happen."* This one is shrewd. Do you sit and wait for somebody to do something and then react? Or, do you act, because it is who you are and what you want to do. Do you take what you want, or wait for permission?

The fourth is by Erma Bombeck: *"It takes a lot of courage to show your dreams to someone else."* That's the real truth. Another way to say that is, it takes guts to put yourself out there, to be vulnerable. Most people just can't do it, so they settle for far less than they really want.

This brings me to a quote by William Shakespeare: *"A coward dies a thousand times before his death, but the valiant taste of death but once."* What about you? Are you ready to throw open the closet doors and expose your real self to the world? Are you ready to boldly go where you dare to dream?

The achievement of a goal, any goal, large or small requires five steps:

1. Set a Noble & Worthy Goal.
2. Think, Build the Plan, Define the Action Steps to Achieve the Goal.
3. Make it Happen, Take Action, Stay Focused,
4. Be Brave, Share Your Talent and Dreams with the World
5. Go for It, Never Give up.

You can have or do anything that you wish as long as you are willing to pay the price. Whenever you are ready, just leap and the net will appear.

80% of Americans have no clear or defined goal, so they just go with the flow. Of the 20% of Americans who do have a goal, most of them do absolutely nothing to move toward it, they just talk, talk, talk.

If you really want to change your life, you must set a goal and then step outside your comfort zone, take the risk, do the work, and stick with it, until you accomplish the mission. You have my permission to start… now!

If you are happy with the way your life is today, then don't change a thing, just stay the course. But, if you want a different result than what you have today, YOU must CHANGE your thoughts, habits and actions. Setting and achieving goals requires CHANGE and that change always begins with YOU! Your new life begins at the edge of your comfort zone.

A Noble Goal 'Must Be' or 'Have' the Following:

- Be Something that you want to do. Not something imposed upon you by another person.
- Be Written. You must write your goal on paper and put it where you will see it every day. You must have the guts to tell the world who you are and what you plan to do! If you can't do that, you have the wrong goal.

- Be Achievable. Impossible goals will only demoralize the team.
- Be Specific. Something like, "I will increase my annual sales by 10%—Twice. From $800K—$880K—$968K. I will earn a 10% Profit. I will take home $96,000."
- Be Measurable. My team will have 100% attendance every week starting now.
- Be Divided into action steps that you and your people can achieve, one small bite at a time. If your goal is to get from 1-10, you start with 1, then 2, then 3, and so on until your get to 10.
- Have a time period. "I'll accomplish this goal by December 31, 2019."
- Have movement. Goals must help you move forward in the right direction, toward the achievement of your mission. You must be able to see and measure the progress every day, week and month.

In addition to you having goals, your people must *also* have goals... Both your goals and the goals of your people must meet the same criteria as above.

Life Balance

This is a book about how to succeed in the restaurant business. If you want to perform at your absolute best, you must be focused, centered and grounded.

It is pointless to have a great business without having people in your life to share your success with. If you want to be truly successful, the business version of you must mesh with the personal, family and community version of you. For that reason, it is important to have goals in four key areas of your life.

1. **Business:** Your Restaurant and Your Investments.
2. **Personal:** Financial, Physical, Social and Spiritual.
3. **Family:** Spouse, Kids, Parents, Siblings and Friends.
4. **Community:** You Must Give Back, Pay It Forward.

If you can get all of your goals to work together, you will have a balanced life. The graphic below shows four balls that represent the different areas of your life.

- On the left, they don't line up, over time, this will cause friction.
- In the center, they overlap like the Olympic rings, much better.
- On the right, the goals stack perfectly. This is great balance.

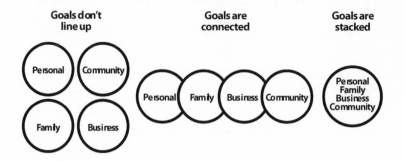

Goals don't line up

Personal · Community · Family · Business

Goals are connected

Personal · Family · Business · Community

Goals are stacked

Personal · Family · Business · Community

You may never get your goals to stack perfectly (mine don't), but with a little intelligent planning, you should be able to get them to work together in harmony. I have a restaurant in a college town, so I hear about life balance every day from young idealists who want (and still think) they can have it all... today.

If you want to build an OK restaurant, you have a much better chance at life balance. If you want to conform and be average, you can have life balance. You may not get rich, but your life will have balance. You may not be happy, but you will have balance.

If you really want to achieve something extraordinary, life balance will have to go out the window. If your goal is to build the best cheeseburger joint in the world, you will probably not achieve life balance. It just isn't possible, especially in the first few years.

Different phases of life require different type of life balance. When you are single, you can work 24 hours a day. When you are married with small children at home, you will need a different focus. When your kids become adults, you can go hard at it again. The point is to find a balance that helps you do your best for you and your family.

Mission vs. Goal

Your Mission is you're your calling. Your reason for living, your purpose in life. The LEADER creates the MISSION, the vision. When thinking of a Mission, Think Big!

President John F. Kennedy wanted to put a man on the moon. Vince Lombardi wanted to win the Super Bowl. Bill Gates saw a PC on every desk. Elon Musk is going to put a man on Mars.

A goal can be abandoned, a MISSION cannot. One of the biggest drawbacks to success is that people keep changing their mission. Winners pick a mission they believe in and stick with it until it is accomplished.

The mission is the umbrella—the big picture. The leader creates the STRATEGY, to achieve the mission. That is what it means when we say "Strategic Thinking".

This book is about Eight Basic Fundamentals. The way to achieve your mission is to set specific goals for each of the eight basic fundamentals and go for them with every ounce of strength and talent that you possess.

Think about that for a minute. First, you need a mission (i.e. - The World's Best Cheeseburger). Then you need specific goals for each of the Eight Basic Fundamentals. The goals will guide you toward the completion of the Mission.

Goals are the incremental steps that we use to accomplish each step of the mission. Departments and individuals will have specific goals to achieve. You must never, ever give up in the quest to achieve your Mission.

Break the goal into steps:

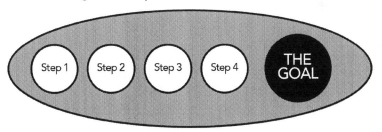

We use tactics to help achieve specific goals. A specific ad campaign is a tactic that the marketing manager uses to increase sales. The strategy will not change very often, but the tactics will change frequently due to current trends, seasonality and financial need.

We develop a strategy to accomplish the mission. We use tactics to achieve incremental goals. Here's how it works:

1. The leader hires a manager to help achieve the *mission*.
2. The leader and manager develop a *strategy* to achieve the *mission*.
3. The manager builds the *team* & creates the *system* to do the work.
4. The manager sets *incremental goals* that lead to the *target*.
5. The individual teams *do the work* to achieve their *individual goals*.
6. Then, the leader *measures* the manager's performance vs. the *goal*.

When the team hits the first goal, the leader and managers work together to set and focus on the next goal or next step. When the team achieves step one, they move on to step two, and then step three, until the MISSION is accomplished.

The leader and manager must be on the same page. You will never win with a weak, indecisive leader or manager at the helm. The worst situation is no leader or too many leaders. You cannot win without a good leader, mission & strategy.

By the way, you are the leader. It's time to get your act together and *lead!*

A Small-Scale Restaurant Owner Example

Imagine, you are a chef. Your wife is a restaurant manager. You are both sick of working for other people, you want your own restaurant. You want the freedom to do your thing. Your plan is to be open for dinner (no lunch) five nights a week. You plan to manage the kitchen; your wife plans to manage the service. You will manage the money, and she will do the marketing.

You find a vacant restaurant space in a decent location that is for rent. You work out a fair rental agreement. The landlord makes some alterations to the space. You cobble together the equipment, and tools. You hire the staff, purchase your opening food and beverage inventory and off you go.

The goal is simple. You plan to earn enough money to live on by operating the restaurant. This can be a good situation provided that one or both of you have a business brain.

The downside is that you and your wife *ARE* the restaurant. If anything bad happens to either of you, the business will fall apart. Your plan is to pay a lot of money and take a huge risk to buy a job.

If you are a restaurant owner who just wants to be a great cook, that's fine but, please be smart enough to find an honest, hard-working business partner who knows how to turn your passion into profit. A 10% Profit.

Pay Attention!

Pay attention to this next paragraph. In fact, read it aloud... Twice!

Good food & drinks are absolutely important. If your food & drinks are not good, you will fail. But food & drinks are only the price of admission. They will only get you into the game.

Good food & drinks are only 20% of the reason that your restaurant will succeed. 80% of your success will be determined by how well you manage and market your restaurant. This is very serious, most (80%) of independent restaurant owners go out of business, because they don't understand this basic concept. A restaurant is a business, a serious business.

A Large Scale Example

Let's imagine the leader sets the goal of creating a National Hamburger Chain called Fresh & Fast! The restaurant will sell three products:

1. Cheeseburgers
2. Fries
3. 20oz Bottles of Coke

Each product will be excellent, there will be no excess steps or grunge to clog the pipe. The operation will be smooth and efficient.

The restaurants will be built on prime real estate. The corporation will buy the real estate and individual restaurants will pay the mortgage and taxes on the properties. The end game is to build 10 stores in ten years, and then sell out to a bigger fish for millions of dollars. This is the Mission and the Strategy to achieve it.

Keep it Short & Simple (K.I.S.S.)

You don't want or need a fancy mission statement that sits in an office drawer collecting dust. JFK didn't have a fancy mission statement for NASA, when he challenged them to send a man to the moon and back.

Next, we bring the mission to life. We do that by setting some goals:

- Goal #1 – Find the person to manage the process. Make a list of qualifications, call a headhunter, and start interviewing.
- Goal #2 – Create the Restaurant Concept
- Goal #3 – Fund the Venture
- Goal #4 – Find the first location. Build the first store.

The first restaurant will have a business plan and financial goals. The management team must work to meet or exceed the financial goals. If you cannot achieve the numbers in store #1, you will never make it to store #2, and the mission will die.

What is the Mission of Your Restaurant?

Why are you in the restaurant business? Why did you start your restaurant? What is or was your DREAM, your VISION, your GOAL? What is the *Financial Goal* of your restaurant?

Did you really start your restaurant to share your Grandmother's meatloaf recipe with the World, or were you looking for the professional freedom to create wealth and financial independence?

Why did you select your current location, food and beverage style, interior design and music style? What was the inspiration for your business venture?

You do not have to tell me your answers. Just think about it, and maybe write your answers on paper.

How long do you expect your restaurant to exist, to live for? Are you building a company that will be handed down to the next generation? Are you building a business to be sold later, so you can cash out and retire? Or, are you just trying to survive this week without going broke?

You Must Be #1 or #2 In Your Market

Your restaurant must be #1 or #2 in your food style or concept category of restaurant. Being the #7 taco joint or pizza place in a market is a recipe for disaster. The smart thing to do is to pick a food or restaurant style *that you know something about and have passion for*. Pick a niche that is being underserved in your market.

Some potential ideas may be:

- Best Cheeseburger, Best Taco or Best Pizza in town.
- Best Italian, French, Thai or Indian Restaurant in town.
- The Best Steak House, Sports Bar, or Food Hall around.

The answers to the questions above should reveal your marketing advantage and central focus of your business. Keep this in mind as you go through the steps of creating the system to deliver the customer experience.

If you are the manager and work for someone else, I suggest that you have a meeting with the owner and get the "answers" to these questions as soon as possible. It's hard to achieve the goal when you don't know what it is.

Pick the Right Project

Be careful what you wish for, because you *will get it*, with all the nasty little strings attached. Smart leaders pick the right project, and get the team focused on the important action steps that lead directly to the target. Spending time on the right things will move you toward success. Spending time on the wrong things is a huge waste of resources that leads to nothing.

If your business is slow, which project would be more important to you? Building an effective marketing campaign, or organizing the spice rack? Both need to be done, but I would work on the marketing campaign and delegate the spice rack to the sous chef.

Some people get more done than others, some people are just busy with bullshit. People who get things done—Survive. People who get the RIGHT things done—Thrive!

Setting Goals

For this conversation, we will limit our focus to the business aspect of your restaurant. I want you to determine the MISSION of your restaurant. What is the real reason your restaurant exists?

Successful people understand that their mission is a long-term quest, not a short-term sprint. Successful people are experts at setting and achieving small daily, weekly and monthly goals that move the team forward toward their ultimate mission.

Winners avoid trivial action and self-destructive behavior that destroys performance. Winners know that a successful life happens by enriching the lives of the people around them, one small step at a time, during this amazing journey of life. 1% better every day, 300% better every year.

Once you have set your goal and defined the steps required to get you from here to there, all you have to do is *focus* on the first step. You simply do your 100% best at the task in front of you today. Do not worry about step #2 or #3, just work on *one thing* at a time.

Always do your best! If your current job or goal does not excite you, get out. Quit. Find something that you love. Life is too short to waste one minute doing something you absolutely hate. Never, cheat yourself, your employees or your employer by doing less than your 100% best. This statement is NOT an excuse to be a quitter; this is simply a challenge to you--a gut check to wake you up and get you moving.

The objective is to do your absolute best at the job in front of you today. When you do this the world will take notice. The people around you will see that you can do excellent work. When you focus on doing your best at everything you do and make it a lifelong habit, it will simply become who you are, and it will become what you are known for.

In addition to focus and effort, your goals and dreams must have a MAGNETIC and GRAVITATIONAL pull. The attainment of your goal must be so strong and desirable in your mind that you cannot imagine living without it. When your goal has magnetic and gravitational pull, it will pull you forward. Your goal will lock onto you, and keep you on course, especially during difficult times.

Yes, there will be distractions and setbacks along the way, there always are. But, when your goal has gravitational and magnetic power, it is much easier to get back up after you fall.

What's Important Now (W.I.N.)

We must spend time on important matters. I love that phrase. It's powerful. In addition to picking the right project we must do the RIGHT Thing. We must focus on the right aspect of the project, the *important* things.

It is vital that you spend your time on important things, not the trivial bullshit. We all have 24 hours in a day. We get to decide how and where we will spend our time. Some people get more things done than others.

Six Levels

There are six different levels of activities that people spend their time on. I want you to start thinking of your time as the most valuable currency on earth. Imagine that you get paid $500 an hour to do the things that move you toward your goal, and you *have to pay* $500 an hour to do the things that move you away from your goal. Wow, doesn't that change your perspective?

The Death Zone: Self Destruction = Cost $500 an Hour

These are self-destructive activities such as gambling, whoring, excessive drinking, doing drugs, and engaging in nefarious activities that lead to physical and mental breakdown. These activities pull you backwards away from your goal. These things can completely de-rail your train.

The death zone also includes things such as taking advantage of people who are smaller and weaker than you. Think about the #MeToo movement, and some of the rich and powerful people like Matt Lauer, Harvey Weinstein and "The Red Menace" who have destroyed their own lives and hurt many other people in the process.

Level One: Time Wasters = Cost $500 an Hour

These are negative personal activities like cigarette breaks, face booking, texting and playing grab ass at work. This includes the DRAMA that spills in from your personal life with things like, calls from collection agents, and psycho ex-wives, girlfriends, husbands and or boyfriends.

Don't forget gossip, backstabbing, personal and inter-department related conflict. These activities are a giant waste of time, talent and money. They lead to, bad attitudes, anger and anxiety. These things pull you and your people sideways and off track. They knock you off the straight and narrow path that leads directly toward the goal. They pull you into the weeds, where *bad things* happen.

Level Two: Setbacks & Distractions = Cost $500 an Hour

These are urgent firefighting issues that pull us sideways such as, covering missed shifts, replacing employees who quit or get fired. They also include equipment breakdowns, printers that don't print, and a myriad of POS issues. These also include surprise visits from the health inspector or fire marshal, ugh. Some of these things are preventable, some are not. Firefighting leads to frustration, stress and burnout. Feel free to add your own list of things to avoid.

Level Three: Doing the Work = Reward $500 an Hour

These activities are both urgent and important. They include operational activities that happen inside the business every day, such as answering the phone, taking reservations, seating guests, running food, cooking, making drinks, turning tables, cleaning and washing dishes.

These are the important things that lead to success and achievement of the goal. These activities can also produce stress and be exhausting when done for long periods of time, without a day off or vacation. The other thing about LEVEL #3 work is you can probably find someone else to do it for less than $500 an hour. This will allow you to focus on the leadership work on Level #4 and #5.

Level Four: Strategic Thinking = Reward $500 an Hour

This is the Strategic Level where we work ON the business system. This includes planning, marketing, management, team building and coaching. Building a great system leads to happiness, victory, financial success and job satisfaction. Great leaders build great systems.

Level Five: The Leadership Level = Reward $1,000 an Hour

Yes, this level is worth $1,000 per hour. This is where we build the next generation of leaders to manage the business. This happens when we have a team of winners. This is the legacy level where true happiness and the beginning stages of life balance happen. This is the goal for all restaurant owners. Build a culture of excellence and teach your people to operate it without you.

Terminator Focus

Do you remember the movie *The Terminator*? The Terminator had one simple mission. Terminate Sarah Connor. The Terminator would make a great restaurant manager, cook or bartender. Imagine what you could accomplish with a team of terminators.

From this moment forward, I want you to think of yourself as a Terminator! Think of your people as an army of terminators. You must train yourself and everyone on your team to be think and act like Terminators.

It is your duty to achieve the goal AND the mission. Any thought or activity that distracts you from achieving your mission must be terminated! Any person who gets in the way of you achieving your goal must be terminated. This is a BIG deal. When your people act like terminators and move the ball forward, everybody wins. There is nothing on Earth that can stop you from achieving your mission. You are a Terminator!

Do Your Job – Hit the Target!

My friend Joe Lee says, don't confuse "Hard Work" with "Results". As the owner of your life, it is your duty to achieve RESULTS. You are not getting paid by the hour. You are being rewarded for what you accomplish.

STOP!

Here is a *big* point... In America, people get paid by the hour. The government says we must pay people a minimum amount for every hour they work. This is a problem because the workforce is motivated by how much they get paid per hour and how many hours they work.

There is a huge difference between simply "Working a lot of Hours" and "Achieving The Desired Results". We can't change the way we pay our people, but we can change the way we measure them.

- Minimum Performance = Minimum Wage
- Great performance = Great Wage

The difference comes down to staying focused on the goal and not accepting failure. This is often referred to as "Working Smart" or being "Effective". Nobody cares how many hours you work. You must take the steps that lead to the GOAL and avoid the ones that don't. We must keep the people who help us achieve the results and replace the people who don't. This is the way the world works, we must play by the rules and do the things that move us toward the goal.

In this book, we will discuss eight basic fundamentals. The point is to use these fundamentals to achieve results, to hit the target and win. Excuses don't cut it. Results do. So, I ask you: Are you hitting your goals, or are you working hard and complaining?

The Plan

Imagine that you have $10,000,000 in the bank and you have just won the best restaurant in the world award. Now What? What's Next?

What would you attempt to do if you had a bottomless credit card that could never run out of money, what would you do all day? If you could go back and do it all over again, what would you do different? Yes, I know you can't go back in time, but you can start implementing your changes starting now and going forward.

Once you know what you want, all you have to do is create a simple plan to achieve it. For example, "I want to go from here to the mall."

Here are the Steps:

1. Get in the car
2. Set the GPS (or tell Siri where you want to go)
3. Drive, follow the plan
4. Arrive at your destination. Boom!

It really is that simple. Your attitude at the beginning of a quest will determine the outcome. Once you set a goal, you simply imagine yourself in possession of it. You proceed as if you already have what you desire. Then you reverse engineer the process from where you want to be "The Goal" back to where you are today.

As we go through this book, I will be asking you to set SMART GOALS for each of the Eight Basic Fundamentals. You will be setting goals for:

- Your Mission or Noble Goal
- Personal Improvement Goals
- Team Building Goals
- Customer Service Goals
- Sales Goals
- Money Management & Profit Goals
- System Development Goals
- Goals to Improve the Improvements

Chapter Recap

The key concepts in this chapter are:

- Set goals for each area: Business, Personal, Family & Community.
- Write your goals down & post where you will see them every day.
- Share your goals with your people.
- Pick the right projects.
- Stick to the mission.
- Terminator focus: never, never, never give up.

Now, while the ideas in this chapter are still fresh in your mind, I want you to answer these simple questions. This should take no more than 10 minutes. You don't have to worry about spelling, grammar, punctuation. Don't put this off, do it NOW! Nothing is more important!

Business Goals
The Mission of My Restaurant is:
The financial goal of my restaurant is:

Personal Goals
My Physical Goal is:
My Spiritual Goal is:
My short-term salary goal is $_____ (think big).
I will have it by this date _____.
My 5-year salary goal is $_____ by this date _____.
I will have $_____ for retirement by the age of _____.

Family Goals
Goal with my spouse:
Goal with my kids:
Goal with my parents:
Goal with friends:

Community Goals
I will do the following for my neighbors:
I will do the following for my Community:

What do You REALLY Want?

Now that you know what your goals are and how to achieve them, I want you to have the guts to go after the ONE goal, the ONE thing that you really, really want. I'm very serious about this. This is a very serious matter.

WHAT do you REALLY want? What does REAL happiness look and feel like to you?

There is no sense in achieving a goal that you don't really want. There is no sense climbing the ladder of success and knowing the entire time that your ladder is on the wrong wall, the wrong building, or the wrong mountain. This would be a terrible waste of time, but people do it all the time. *You know what I'm talking about, right?*

I'm not talking about what you are willing to SETTLE for. I'm talking about what you really want. I'm talking about the ONE thing that wakes you up in the middle of the night. The one thing that you'll go through hell to get.

Who are YOU and WHY are you here? What do YOU want? Write that down… because that is your *real* goal. Now, I want you to write 10 Things that you can do to achieve your goal:

Fundamental #2:
Develop the Owner's Mindset

I am an Iowa Hawkeye football fan. I feed the players, coaches and staff four times every week. I feed them when they win and when they lose. I know how hard they work. They are my heroes. The quote below is from the greatest Iowa Hawkeye football player of all time:

"Give me the courage and ability to so conduct myself in every situation that my country, my family and my friends will be proud of me."

- Nile Kinnick, Jr., 1941

This message is for every restaurant owner, manager, chef, bartender, line cook, server, and even the CEO of a large restaurant group. This fundamental is all about you. Developing the Owner Mindset is the first step in your transformation. The truth is that we can't fix anything until we get you headed in the right direction.

I'm sure that you have heard many of these ideas and concepts before, but this time I want you to actually incorporate them into your life. I want you to live them. These are the magic formulas to success on this planet. If you do them, you will win. If not, you will continue to lose.

Take Ownership & Do Your Job 100% +1%

This is serious business. You're responsible for millions of dollars and the lives of every person who works in your restaurant. This fundamental is about taking ownership of your life and your destiny. The key word here is— TAKE.

Leaders (TAKE) responsibility for their lives and the actions and performance of the entire team. Leaders do not blame other people for their failure. Leaders share the victories and take full responsibility for the failure. Winners know that failure is only a temporary set-back. Winners NEVER, EVER Give Up.

Failure in the restaurant business is a very real and unpleasant option. Failure will destroy your family and the family of everyone who works for you. It is your duty, to perform to the best of your ability and do everything in your power to keep the team moving forward. It's your duty to win.

You must do your job 100% plus the *"Magic 1%"*. This means that you must do your job, then add something extra to your performance every day. You must find a small way to improve every day.

Imagine that you run one mile in six minutes every day. Imagine that the guy across the street does the same thing. Now imagine that you add an extra 15 feet to your run every day. In one year, you will be running two miles a day, and the guy across the street will still be running one mile. In two years, you will be running three miles every day. In two years, you will become three times better than your competition. Now imagine the opposite: Your competitor becomes three times stronger and better than you. Wow! *It's time to add the Magic 1%.*

Self-Reliance

The concept of self-reliance is pretty simple. It means that you rely mostly on yourself. It means you have the means to support yourself, you don't need a free pass, a handout, or welfare to get by. Self-Reliance means that when you want something, you go get it!

Self-Reliant people own their lives, and they have the "Owners Mindset". You must have the "Owner Mindset", you must own the outcome and the result. It is your duty to make things happen. You must be self-reliant.

As the owner you are in charge of your life, your restaurant and your team. Everything that goes wrong is 100% your fault! You cannot blame your people for your failure. You must accept the truth and the failure. You can't blame your people for making mistakes, you must train them to win or find other people who can.

The next time you find yourself complaining about someone who screwed up... Stop and blame yourself. If you really want to find the person who is screwing things up, go look in the mirror. You are the one who hired them and didn't train them.

If the work in your restaurant is too hard or too complicated for average human beings with average skills, maybe you have the wrong concept? Maybe you need to re-think what YOU are asking your people to do. Stop blaming others for your weakness and deficiencies. Yes, it is your restaurant, your job and your fault! So, fix it!

The Owner Mindset is the exact opposite of the self-entitlement syndrome. Self-Entitled people believe the world owes them a living. Self-entitled people never accept responsibility, they avoid tough problems, they kick the problem up the ladder to the manager, the leader, or the owner.

Self-entitled, small thinkers play the blame game, they guard their turf, they deflect responsibility, and always have a ready excuse, because nothing is ever their fault. Small thinkers need someone else to do the real thinking and make the tough decisions for them. Small people love to piss and moan to their fellow employees. Self-Entitled people kill restaurants! You are not entitled to anything. If you want something, you must EARN it!

Have you ever wondered how great leaders and winners come up with the great ideas, that solve problems and move the ball forward? It's really quite simple:

Smart Owners and Leaders THINK BIG, they TAKE charge of their lives, they know what they want, and they TAKE it. Great leaders take ownership of every situation and focus on finding the BEST LONG-TERM SOLUTION.

Winners ask themselves the following questions every day:

- How can I add value to, and improve the customer experience?
- How can I add value & help my people improve their performance?
- How can I add value & help the business thrive over the long term?
- How are people going to do this in 10 or 20 years from now?
- How can we do this thing smarter than we are doing it today?
- What is the best way to solve this problem, and add real value for everyone involved?
- What is the ONE thing, I can do right now, that will move us to a better place or solution?

As the owner, it is your responsibility to improve the customer experience, the performance of every person on your team and the profitability of your restaurant. You must seek and find the best ideas and long-term solutions, not the most politically expedient answer or short-term quick fix.

Reality Check #1

Your life is the way it is because of YOU and your thinking. You are the sum-total of every thought you have ever had and every action you have ever taken in your life. If you are not happy with where you are today, all you have to do is start making better decisions. You must accept responsibility and face the truth—No excuses. This is your life… You are the one who is writing the script. It is up to you to make things happen the way you want them to.

Reality Check #2

You will never win with small thinkers and losers on your team. You must replace the people who have self-entitlement syndrome with winners and self-starters, who will help you move forward to victory. If you want something, you must get off your ass and go get it. You must take the bull by the horns and create the life of your dreams. You are not entitled to anything.

Reality Check #3

This is the BEST time in the history of the world to be alive, and the future will be even better. The world is getting safer and better every day. Sure, there is bad news, but the majority is good. You have so many great advantages that your forefathers could only dream of. Opportunity is everywhere, it is up to you to choose a goal and make it happen. Yes, America is filled with entitled people, it is an epidemic and that is good news for you. It should be very easy to get ahead of the weaklings who have self-entitlement syndrome.

Reality Check #4

The World wants you to THRIVE and become RICH! It is your duty to build wealth for you and your family. People get rich by adding value to other people's lives. My man, Zig Ziglar said, "You can have anything you want, as long as you are willing to give enough other people what they want." Rich people are rich because they stay focused on the goal and add value to the lives of many, many people. What value are you adding?

A wealthy business owner can reward her people better than the owner who is just scraping by. Look around your market, the restaurants that provide the best food, drinks, service and value to the community are THRIVING. And the restaurants that provide a mediocre product and marginal service, are closing.

Being rich is a blessing, not a curse. The world wants you to be rich, so you can improve the lives of your family, friends, employees and community. It is your responsibility to be prosperous, so you can provide an excellent lifestyle and education for yourself and your family. If you are the restaurant owner, it is your duty to make your business thrive. If you are a manager or team member, it is your duty to help the company thrive.

People who do their job 100% and move the company forward, get the reward. People who do the minimum and hold the company hostage, get replaced. There is no middle ground. You are either moving the company forward, or you are holding us back!

Better People Build Better Restaurants

If you want to have a better life, you must become a better person. Character and integrity are the bedrock of success. This is not some obligatory entry into a book. This is the most important step in the process of building a restaurant that will stand the test of time. You cannot build a long- term success story by being a shithead, a liar, and a thief. You must have a strong moral foundation to build an organization of value. Think of George Washington vs. Bernie Madoff, and you'll get the idea. The goal is to become a better version of yourself every day:

- Why do people go to school? To become better educated.
- Why do people go to the gym? To get in better shape.
- Why do people quit smoking? To have better health.

We can exchange the word BETTER for the word EXCELLENCE. When we strive for excellence, we move forward to a better life. This means we should strive for EXCELLENCE in everything we do. Excellence means doing the right thing—the right way—every time. Excellence requires courage and a clear understanding of the mission. Excellence requires the guts to stay the course and do the right thing—even when no one is watching.

"We are what we repeatedly do. Excellence then, is not and act, but a habit."

- Aristotle

Think about the three most successful people that you know, what do they all have in common? I will bet they all have four qualities in abundance—character, focus, perseverance and self-reliance.

Goal #1 is to become a better version of yourself every day. Here's how you can put it to work:

Just pick one of the *Eight Basic Fundamentals*, (start with the one that needs the most improvement) select any aspect of that fundamental and find a way to improve it by 1%. You can start with anything from improving the message on a table tent to the way you clean the corners of your bathroom floors. That's right! Go into your bathroom and look at the corners of the floor. That will tell you how clean your restaurant really is.

If you improve one aspect of your restaurant by 1% every day, just think how far ahead you will be in one month or one year. If you can get your managers and team members to do the same thing, your restaurant will see an exponential growth and transformation in the next 90 days!

The Goal is 1% Better Every Day!

Better people do a better job. Better people become better cooks. Better people become better bartenders. Better people become better waiters. Better people become better managers and leaders. Better people also become better parents, aunts, uncles, brothers, sisters, friends and neighbors. Better People Build Better Restaurants and Better Lives.

A strong character and moral fiber are the first two ingredients in building a Great Restaurant. Our character is shaped by our virtues and values:

- Virtues are the moral standards that we live by, this is also called moral fiber.
- Values are the things that you and your organization consider vital to the mission.

Remember this, a strong character is more important than knowledge and talent.

Better People Make Better Cooks, Bartenders, Waiters, and Managers.

Honesty + Integrity + Authenticity + Resilience = Performance

Think about George Washington, Benjamin Franklin and Thomas Jefferson. They were the founders of our country. They gave birth to a nation that they would never get to enjoy. They did the hard work, and 240+ years later we get to enjoy the fruits of their labor.

It's the same thing with your restaurant, you are a founding member—it is your duty to create a legacy of excellence for future generations to follow.

Above or Below the Line Decisions

This concept comes from two of my favorite books, *The OZ Principle* and *The Slight Edge*. In this section, I will whisk them together, and add my own twist.

Your attitude has a direct effect on your decisions, actions and behavior. Your actions and behavior will determine your performance and eventual success or failure. Every situation in life will present you with two options.

Do the Right Thing or Don't Do the Right Thing

The right thing is:

1. Easy to do.
2. Easy to NOT do.

When your alarm clock goes off at 5:30 am, do you hit snooze, smoke a bong and go back to bed, or do you get up, take a shower, brush your teeth, put on clean clothes and go to work? Do you focus on the important things that move you toward the goal or waste time on trivial matters?

Did you do your job, plus the magic 1% today? Do you do everything the right way, or are you satisfied with the OK way? Do you finish your work 100%, or leave it for the next guy to deal with?

Making the positive decision is easy to do, and it is also easy not to do. When you think and act positively your performance will continually improve, which will eventually lead you to success. When you think and act negatively, your performance will decline—which will eventually lead to failure. The diagram below shows a black line with <u>positive</u> attitude, behavior and action above the line, and <u>negative</u> attitude, behavior and action below the line.

Over-time, POSITIVE thinking and action will improve your performance and send you to the stars. Over-time, negative thinking and action will hurt your performance and send you into the downward spiral of doom & gloom.

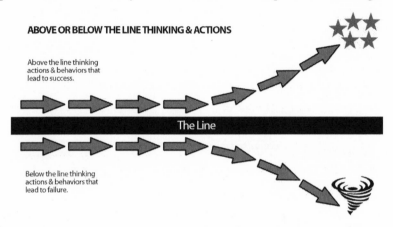

ABOVE OR BELOW THE LINE THINKING & ACTIONS

Above the line thinking actions & behaviors that lead to success.

The Line

Below the line thinking actions & behaviors that lead to failure.

Up & Down—Positive & Negative

We all have good days and bad days. Our attitude and behavior go up and down between positive and negative. Some people kick ass one day and completely dog it the next day. Most people jump from one idea to another, or change the concept mid-stream, they never stick with anything long enough to work out the problems and build positive momentum.

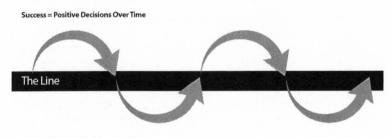

Success = Positive Decisions Over Time

The Line

Failure = Negative Decisions Over Time

It comes down to making the right decisions. The people who really win, stay focused and make the right decision. They do the right thing every single time, every single day. Making the right decision is very easy to do, but so is taking the shortcut and making the wrong decision.

Your Attitude

A positive attitude is the single most important thing you have. If you want to win you must keep your attitude above the line. How long can you go without allowing a negative thought to push your attitude below the line? 10 seconds, 30 seconds, 10 minutes, one day, one week? Remember, we become what we think about.

Your attitude drives your thoughts and your thoughts drive your behavior and action. I encourage you to start paying attention to your attitude, it is the *real force* that is driving your life. The good news is that we get to choose our attitude and the bad news is we get to choose our attitude.

Your situation does NOT choose your attitude. Your people do not choose your attitude. Your customers do not choose your attitude... you do!

Think about your actions and behaviors. Do you spend your time working on the POSITIVE above the line activities that will move your restaurant and your life forward or do you spend your time on negative below the line bullshit that drives you crazy? Are you being problem-focused? Or opportunity-focused? Is your glass half empty or half full?

The Winners Victory Party is happening above the line. The losers pity party is happening below the line. Above the line is happiness, joy, and victory. Below the line is self-entitlement, misery, self-destruction, and death.

I want you to spend 100% of your time on POSITIVE things that will move your life forward. Today, when you walk into work, I want you to find something positive to work on, I want you to broadcast a positive message to your team and everyone you come in contact with. Can you do that? You don't need to fake it until you make it. Just find something *good* and focus on that.

Here's the point: 80% of the things that are happening in your restaurant are GOOD and only 20% are BAD. The same is true for your life. When we spend all our time on the 20% that is bad, we totally miss the best part of life! I want you to FLIP this. I want you to focus on the 80% of your restaurant and your life that is good. I want you to find ways to improve the 80% that is good.

Do you know the phrase "As long as I'm yelling at you, you are good, and when I stop yelling at you, you're dead"? It's time to stop yelling at the losers, just replace them with winners!

Find positive people who want to have fun and help you build your restaurant into a cult brand. Seek and find positive people who want to win! Remember, we become what we think about. The process starts with you. Think positive & win!

80% of restaurants owners and managers live between failure and survival. One day they wake up and realize they are failing and vow to try harder. They improve their attitude and start making better decisions, which improves their behavior and performance. Before long, their situation improves, and they move from the failure line to the survival line.

But, as soon as they reach the survival line, they breathe their first 'sigh of relief' then return to the sloppy self-entitled attitude and behavior that got them in trouble in the first place.

Before long they find themselves right back at the failure line, sucking wind. For 80% of all restaurants this process repeats itself, over and over again. *That's 8 out of 10 restaurants.*

The Top 15%

The Top 15% of restaurants stay focused. They maintain their positive attitude and actions for a long time. They make the small positive decisions that improve their performance. Before long they have a breakthrough and move up from failure, to survival, and if they stay with it long enough, they will eventually hit the success level.

The Top 5%

The Top 5% of Restaurants keep at it until they reach the Thrive Level! These owners and managers make positive attitude and actions the habit of a lifetime. They work on the Eight Basic Fundamentals and consistently make the small decisions that improve their performance.

These people do their job 100% then add the Magic 1% every day.

5% of all restaurant owners are thriving and living the lives of their dreams. This can & will happen to you when you get focused on the *Eight Basic Fundamentals* and consistently make the small, positive decisions that lead to your goal. This simple idea will work every time and yes, it will even work for you. You CAN do it! I'll show you how.

The Flip Side

Now that you know your goal is to build a place for winners to thrive, here's the flip side. You must drive out the losers and people with "self-entitlement syndrome". Winners hate working with losers and losers hate working with winners.

Who do you want to build your team with? Winners or losers? You can't have both; a blend of both is a recipe for disaster and death! You must choose one or the other.

Phronesis, Virtuous Action

Here's a little wisdom from Aristotle:

Leadership requires excellence. Excellence requires courage without being afraid or overly cautious, and a clear understanding of the pitfalls & dangers involved in any undertaking.

Leadership is personal. The first victory for a leader is to master him or herself. A leader must have the personal fortitude and strength to rule over their personal desires. The leader must avoid shame or disgrace. A fool cannot be a leader!

Leadership is social. The leader is an integral part of the team and community, not an isolated individual. The leader must exhibit personal and professional excellence among the team members. The leaders must rise up from the ranks and be lifted by the people, the members of the team.

The team must first accept the leader as a member of the group, and then, raise him up! The people must look up to the leader and accept his rule. The people must want to protect their virtuous leader. The leader must not be a tyrant, or a ruthless prick; otherwise, the people will destroy or leave him.

Leadership is moral. The leader must focus with moral authority on the goal and the mission. The best and most excellent leaders set the moral standard to be lived up to and followed. The leader must expect courage and high moral standards from every member of the leadership team.

The BIGGEST danger of leadership is not physical, it's moral. Loss of moral leadership is a fate worse than death. The leader must be the most excellent in all ways. The leader must set the standard of excellence to be followed. The leader must be the highest Moral Authority.

Leadership is paternal/maternal. Think of a virtuous father or mother teaching and watching out for their children and loved ones. The entire leadership team must behave in this manner.

Strong restaurants are run by the leader--not by the people, because the leader is the BEST equipped to make decisions and lead. At least he or she better be. The real leader on any team of value is the one who sets the standard for excellence and exhibits the highest level of moral authority.

The 9-Dot Puzzle

The 9-Dot Puzzle has been around for centuries. It goes all the way back to the Egyptians, who used ladybugs in the desert sand to create the nine dots. It is an awesome brain teaser. It is considered by many people smarter than me to be the origin of "outside-the-box thinking". The objective is:

- Connect all nine dots below
- Using a pen or pencil
- With only four straight lines
- You cannot lift the pen from the paper

The 9 Dot Puzzle

Yes, this problem is solvable! Please spend some time thinking about it before you give up and go find the answer. This is a great test in self-reliance. You have the power inside your brain to solve it!

This problem involves creative, outside-the-box thinking. You must let go of your preconceived ideas and OPEN YOUR MIND to new possibilities. You will have to step back and see the BIG picture.

If you do find the answer, by yourself, you will be very pleased with yourself, it will build confidence. Give this problem some time before you give up and cheat. I put the answer in chapter eight, because I know that you will be tempted to just turn the page, to find the answer--which is what most people do, they give up and try to find the answer on Google.

Please use your brain, try to solve this by yourself, before you give up and look. This is a test of your power to THINK! This problem requires the same type of creative thinking that is required to solve the problems in your restaurant

You *can* do it! If you are willing to open your mind, see the big picture and think outside the box. Before you give up and look for the answer, get your team together and see if they can help you solve it. This can be an excellent team-building exercise.

Chapter Recap

The key points in developing the owner mindset are:

- Do your job 100%, plus the Magic 1%.
- Be self-reliant.
- Face reality.
- Develop & share your values.
- Become a better version of you.
- Positive above the line thinking & actions.
- Phronesis, virtuous action.
- Open your mind and think outside the box.

While the ideas in this section are fresh in your mind. I want you to write your goal for personal improvement.

Then I want you to make a list of 10 THINGS that you can do to improve. 10 things that will help you become a better version of yourself. This should take no more than 10 minutes. Chances are that you already know what you need to improve. Don't put this off, do it NOW! Nothing is more important as improving your life.

This Is Your First Test. This exercise is EASY TO DO and EASY NOT TO DO. It's time to decide—right here, right now—are you willing to change?

When I grow up, I want to have these qualities in abundance:

My goal for personal improvement is:

I will do the following 10 things to improve:

Fundamental # 3:
Build A Winning Team

Imagine, it's a rainy day with thunder boomers and lightning strikes everywhere. Imagine, that you are the pilot of an airplane. When you first take off the rain is pounding your plane. When you enter the clouds it gets bumpy, really bumpy. When you get above the clouds, the sun is shining and it's smooth sailing.

Life is Good.

My goal is to help you get yourself and your entire team up and above the clouds, where good things happen, and it is possible to enjoy life and achieve your dreams.

The goal of most people and most restaurant owners and managers is to take off and fly to their destination at a comfortable altitude. The problem is most people (95%) spend all their time in the "weather of the day". When it's nice and sunny, all is well. When it's a rainy and nasty, you get hammered by the rain and bumped about by the clouds. If your team cannot get above the clouds, eventually it will be torn apart by turbulence and crash to the ground in a gigantic fireball of death.

Think of your people as little airplanes. Where are they on their flight plan? Are they on the tarmac ready to take off? Are they just lifting off, getting pelted by the rain? Are they in the clouds getting pounded by turbulence and struck by lightning? Or, are they above the clouds, sailing smoothly in the sunshine?

Every time you hire a new employee, the process starts again, every new employee must start at takeoff and climb through the rain and clouds into the sunshine.

1. Prepare for Takeoff = The Interview & Hiring Stage
2. Take Off = Rain = Learning & Training
3. In the Clouds = Figuring it Out
4. Above the Clouds = Moving the Ball Forward

Now, think about the performance of your team. I bet most of the time you and your people live in the weather of the day, sometimes nice and smooth, sometimes really bumpy. The objective is to train yourself and your team to find a way to win in any kind of weather. This requires the desire, talent and ability to get above the clouds quickly.

Most restaurant teams are made up of part-time people, and they have very high turnover, which means the owner and managers are always on the tarmac, trying to help the newbies take off and navigate through the rain and clouds.

The secret, as you know, is to work with your people to teach & coach them, so they can get safely above the clouds where good things happen. We must surround ourselves with full-time long-term team members who have the interest to get above the clouds.

We must surround ourselves with people who have talent, or at least the interest and ability to develop talent, and perform at a high level. When I speak about "high level", I am talking about getting and staying above the clouds where life is great. Above the clouds where winners live.

The goal of this chapter is to show you the steps involved in building a winning team. A winning team that wants to fly far above the clouds and live among the BEST in the world. Doesn't that sound good? The World's Best? What's the point of playing the game, if you don't want to improve, grow and become your best?

Why Would Anyone Want to Work for You?

Here is a great question.: What makes you worthy of being their leader, coach, and mentor?

If you are thinking that people are lucky to have a job in this economy— Think Again! Your answer cannot be money, good people need much more than money. This is a free agent nation and people with character, knowledge and talent can work anywhere they want to. Just because you are the owner, manager or chef, of a restaurant doesn't mean that anyone should want to follow you. I am not talking about hiring ignorant, warm bodies who can barely fog a mirror. I'm talking about creating a culture of excellence where *winners* thrive!

Winners are looking for OPPORTUNITY! Winners want to work with other winners, at a place where they can grow, improve their knowledge and skills and make a real contribution. Winners want to work for a GREAT COACH, LEADER and MENTOR, who can inspire them to aim for the stars, and become far more than they are today. So, I ask you again, why would anyone ever want to work for you?

Here are a few questions that 'winners' need you to answer before they will join your team:

- What's in it for me? Why would I want to leave my current job and come to work for you?
- What is the overt benefit of working for you? (for instance: cool projects, great pay, career advancement, real experience, resume builder, unique opportunity)
- What is the dramatic difference between working for you? Working for my current boss? Or the four other restaurant owners who want me?
- What is the reason that I should believe you? What have you—or your restaurant—done lately that makes this a great place for me? Who have you taught and mentored that has gone on to real success, and when can I talk to them?

Remember this—In addition to potential job candidates, asking these questions during an interview, your current employees are asking themselves these questions every morning before they come to work, and then again, every time you act like an ass-hat and piss them off.

The Employee Experience

Everybody is talking about the customer experience, what about the "employee experience"? Ask yourself these questions:

- What are you doing for your people?
- How are you helping them grow and prosper?
- How does your training program and culture help them move forward and thrive?
- How do you and your managers make working in your restaurant a fun and rewarding experience?

The goal is to create a culture of excellence where winners thrive. You must create an environment that attracts the best people that your market has to offer. Your restaurant must be the place where the best people want to work. You must empower your winners and let them grow. Challenge them to improve and grow as people and professionals. Our competitive advantage is our Culture of Excellence!

A Culture of Excellence

Creating the right culture is the job of the leader. The goal is to create a Culture of Excellence where all your people are professional restaurant operators who strive to deliver the customer promise and become a better version of themselves every day.

Creating and shaping a culture is a big deal. Your restaurant will develop a very specific culture and it is going to happen with or without you. When you break it down, culture is simply "the way we do things here". The culture of your restaurant is the thing that makes it EXACTLY what it is today. It is YOUR JOB to decide what you want your specific culture to be and then show your people what it looks like.

I'm going to start with a wide view of culture and then zoom in to the specific culture your restaurant. There are many different types of cultures.

There are Macro Cultures: Countries have macro cultures. Think of the huge differences between America, France, China, Russia, India, and North Korea. Even within America, there are big cultural differences: people raised in Brooklyn are wired differently than people raised in Berkley.

There are Micro Cultures: Different professions have different cultures, sometimes these cultures transcend national and ethnic boundaries. Lawyers, Doctors, Engineers, Accountants, NFL Football Players, Navy Seals, Musicians and Plumbers all have different cultures.

There is Personal & Families Culture: People from different backgrounds have a different point of view, they interpret things differently. People who grew up in the south during the 50's and 60's see things differently than someone who grew up in the Midwest in the 90's. There are differences between people who grew up wealthy and people who grew up poor. Rich kids often make better salespeople, because they think nothing of recommending a $100 bottle of wine, while a poor or middle-class kid, would find it more difficult.

Then, there is General Restaurant Culture: Every restaurant has Kitchen Culture, Management Culture and Dining Room Culture. There are Owners, Chefs, Managers, Bartenders, Waiters and Dishwashers who all have their own mindset and culture. The schedule is a perfect example of this, I can laminate my kitchen schedule and not change it for three months, while it's almost impossible to get the waiters to stick to the schedule for two weeks without making changes. Chefs are notorious for screaming and yelling but, it would be a real surprise for a 20-year old hostess to blow a gasket and start throwing stuff.

There is Specific Restaurant Culture: There are cultural differences between restaurants. The culture difference between a sushi restaurant and a burger joint is huge! The culture in a McDonald's is much different than the culture of Pizza Hut, which is different from Bern's Steakhouse in Tampa or The French Laundry in Napa.

Your Restaurant has a Culture: If you are a good leader and you have a clear vision and goals, the culture of your restaurant is shaped by you, then it is followed by your managers, then adopted by your employees, and--if your culture is really cool--your customers will jump on board, too. But, if you are not a good leader and do not have a clear vision and goals, the culture of your restaurant will be shaped by the waiters and cooks. Once culture is set, it is VERY difficult to change.

Your Service Culture is being created by your Dining Room Manager, during the daily staff meeting (if they have one) and through every interaction your people have with him or her. Your Culinary Culture is being created by your Chef and Sous Chef. Your cooks are following their lead.

The question is WHAT message are your managers feeding the staff? Are they following your lead, and sharing your vision or are they just showing up and going through the motions? If you don't provide direction, your people will find their own.

The true culture of your restaurant is what happens when you are NOT there! Sit back and think about this. What happens when you are not there? Are your people focused on achieving the goal or do they play grab ass, drink your booze and rob you blind? Wow!

Your restaurant is like a giant petri dish, and the culture is growing every day. The BIG question is WHAT type of nutrients and nourishment are your people being fed and who is feeding them? Are they being fed crap by their misguided peers, or are they being fed a positive vision and the inspiration of something greater than themselves?

In 80% of all restaurants, the real culture is being shaped by the employees! That's right, the real culture of your dining room is being shaped while the waiters are rolling silverware and standing around in the side stations.

The real culture of your restaurant is being shaped by the cook with the biggest mouth or the best drugs. The real culture of your restaurant is being created in the office by your managers when you are NOT THERE!

There are five steps of creating a culture. Every new idea must go through all five steps before it becomes a permanent part of your culture.

1. Assumption
2. Belief
3. Acceptance
4. Expectation
5. Artifact

Assumption

The leader introduces a new idea to the system with the assumption that it will work. For example, let's imagine the leader sets a new standard of 100% Attendance for every shift.

Belief

After one week, the staff shows up on time for every shift. The managers & staff will begin to believe that it can happen again, and maybe all the time.

Acceptance

The managers and staff must accept the idea. You can't just ram it down their throats, you must use your powers of persuasion to help your people see the merit and value of a new idea. We all have a built-in system that wants things to stay the way they are, you must to be patient and help your people work through change.

Expectation

After several months of everybody being on time, your people will expect it to happen all the time. 100% Attendance will become an expectation of the team and part of the CULTURE! Payday is a great example of an expectation. If your people don't get paid, there will be blood!

Artifact

The artifact is the PHYSICAL PROOF that the idea exists. A Great Schedule with NO missed shifts is an artifact. Your P&L with a lower food cost is an artifact. An increased check average is an artifact. Money in the bank is a great artifact. Every new idea must go through all five phases. Ideas must be accepted and embraced by the team before they become part of the culture.

FIVE STEPS OF CULTURE

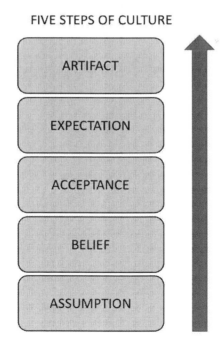

Company Values

This is a big one. Having solid values and sharing them with your team will help keep everybody on the same page. Knowing what your COMPANY VALUES are will be very helpful when you and your team are faced with a tough decision. We use these values as a template to measure employee candidates during the interview and audition process. Our values guide us through the vicissitudes of life. What does your company truly value? For inspiration, here are my company values:

- Positive Attitude: Have Fun & Enjoy life!
- Great Relationships with customers, team members & suppliers.
- Great Food & Drinks: Quality, Craftsmanship, Consistency.
- Hospitality: Make the customer feel Special & Important.
- Customer Focused: Deliver the Customer Promise.
- Personal Improvement: 1% every day.
- Truth & Honesty: Tell the Truth the first time.
- Say/Do Ratio: We do what we say we will do.
- Availability: Full-Time people who see the restaurant business as a long-term career.
- 100% Attendance: We are here on time, ready for every shift.
- Do Your Job 100%: Hit the numbers, no excuses.
- Pac Man: The people who DO the most, GET the most.
- Stair-Step Training: Start at the beginning and work your way up.
- The System: We define the way we do things here.
- Cleanliness & Sanitation: Our restaurant is "Surgical Clean".
- Organization: Everything is always in the RIGHT place.
- Reduce Waste for the business and the planet.
- Sales > Expenses: Spend 10% less than we earn.
- Hunger & Drive: We have passion for our people & products.
- Perseverance: We will Never, Never, Never Give Up!

You must let every person on your team know what you value as an organization. People who share your VALUES will stay with you for a LONG TIME, people who do not, will slither away quickly!

If you want to be successful, you must hire people with character. This means hard working people with guts and moral fiber. You cannot build a winning team of wimps, drunks, and potheads.

"We rarely fire people for performance-related infractions. It always comes down to a major character flaw."

- Evan Harman

Recruiting

Here is a word we don't use enough in the restaurant business: Recruiting. We hear hiring and firing all the time, but rarely recruiting. I am going to suggest that RECRUITING is the single most important word in the restaurant business. If people are our number one asset, then finding and getting them to join our team, is the first and most important step in the process.

My question is—how much time do you and your managers spend recruiting the next generation of players? I'm not talking about putting ads on Craigslist and Facebook. I'm talking about taking the process to the next level.

Be a Great Recruiter. Finding *great* people is a full-time job. If you have ever advertised for a cook or waiter, you have probably noticed that there are very few qualified candidates who apply. There are two reasons for this phenomenon,

1. Only 5% of the cook, waiter, bartender or manager market is actively looking for a job this very moment.
2. 80% of all applicants are "unemployable. In other words, they are the wrong fit.

This is why most restaurant operators think—Good people are hard to find. The fact is, that good people ARE hard to find... when we need them.

My restaurants have very high standards and expectations. I find that for every 100 applications that we receive, only 1% of the people will make it from application to the 90-Day of employment point. Most of the people that we hire, look and sound good up front, but over time they lack the drive and determination to do the work, so they wash out quickly. This is why we are ALWAYS recruiting and looking for our next great player.

Hire Like A Sports GM, Not An HR Director

Most human resource directors and restaurant managers suck at hiring. I want you to think about how your restaurant hires people. Do you hire the *best* people in the market, or do you do you hire warm bodies who are just looking for a job? It's true, most restaurant managers hate posting jobs and sifting through applications, there has to be a better way!

Professional Sports Managers are all about TALENT!

I see hiring as the most important fundamental of building a winning team and a great restaurant. I want you to change your mindset and start thinking like the GM of a professional sports team.

The General Manager of a professional sports team is dedicated to ONE THING, finding and hiring the BEST talent available. The best GM's win the most championships, because they have the BEST people! It really is that simple!

Think of great restaurateurs like Thomas Keller and Danny Meyer, they have great restaurants because they have the best people in the industry. Every culinary school and restaurant management school graduate wants to work for them. They get to pick from the BEST people the market has to offer. Imagine what you could accomplish with a team of winners who are driven to produce excellent results.

Most restaurant managers are used to being short staffed and desperate to find a warm body to fill the schedule. The hardest part of team building is not when you are desperate and short-handed, but when you have a full team of good players, and a really good player shows up looking for a job.

When someone who is better than one of your current players, shows up looking for a job, you MUST hire them. This will force you to CUT your weakest player, someone who is good, but not as good as the new guy.

This is a very difficult concept for most managers to grasp, because they have never had to cut a good player before. This is the moment of truth, bring in the "star", or keep the "OK" guy. We will discuss this in detail in the evaluation chapter.

You must hire:

- Cooks who have a solid work ethic who "get off" on great food.
- Bartenders who are honest, make drinks to our standards and keep the bar clean.
- Servers who can sell, love people & deliver the customer promise.
- Hostesses who are intelligent, dress well, & make our customers feel special & important.

Your Job Is To Build a Winning Team

You will do that by creating a great recruiting system to attract the best talent in your market.

Pigs and Chickens

Who gave more to the breakfast meal of bacon and eggs? The pig or the chicken? Here's a fun story, with important meaning:

A pig and a chicken are walking down the road. They see a sign and notice that a potluck breakfast was under way. Caught up in the moment, the pig suggested to the chicken that they each make a contribution.

"Great idea," said the chicken. "Let's offer them bacon & eggs!"

"Not so fast." The pig said. "For you, that's just a contribution, but for me, it's a total commitment!"

Let me ask you, are you a pig or a chicken? How about your managers?

In Food Guru World we have "team members". We do not have employees. Our team members are divided into two groups: pigs and chickens.

Pigs Live to Work

Pigs give 100% every day. Pigs have the OWNER MINDSET. They are in it to win it. When the restaurant has a big day, the pigs are here, grinding it out. When an employee quits, the pigs cover the open shifts. Pigs adjust their personal life to fit their work life. Pigs never just stand around. You never have to tell a pig to find something to do. Pigs make a big contribution, every single day. Pigs are here to win. Pigs Rule!

Chickens Work to Live

Chickens make a valuable contribution, and they do a good job (when they are here). Chickens love being on the team, they love the job, they do the work and go home. When things are slow, chickens will stand around, (talk shit) and watch the pigs work. Chickens have no problem requesting off on New Year's Eve, Mother's Day or anytime something fun comes up in their *real life*.

Chickens often *say* they want to be pigs, they might even act like pigs for a short time, just to get a raise, don't get sucked in. The big difference between pigs and chickens is, pigs move the ball forward every day, chickens talk about moving the ball forward.

Sometimes the chickens help the pigs move the ball forward. This happens because the pigs make them help—the pigs *forced* them to do it. This is why the chickens sometimes *think* they moved the ball forward. But, left on their own, they would have never made the extra effort.

There is nothing wrong with having chickens on your team, just don't expect anything extra from them, because they will always disappoint you, especially when you are desperate. Team members can be chickens, but managers must be pigs!

Employees

Employees are here to collect a paycheck. Employees are here for a J.O.B. Employees steal, show up late, and do the minimum necessary to survive. Employees need a babysitter *and* a supervisor. Employees will gossip, suck the clock, and distract the pigs, which creates pissed off pigs!

Caution: Chickens and Employees usually expect the same reward (pay) as the Pigs for far less performance. Don't get sucked in. Be smart, measure the performance of your people and post the results, so everybody can see where they stack up. Never candy coat the truth, be honest with your people and let them know their reward will be based on performance, not friendship.

The moral of the story is. You must build a TEAM of WINNERS. You must reward the PIGS with the best money, shifts, benefits and perks. You must surround yourself with PIGS. You must let the chickens know that they are important to the mission and keep them moving toward the goal. Most importantly, you must replace self-entitled employees with hard working, dedicated pigs!

Play Pacman

In the game Pac Man, the goal is to move around the screen eating stuff and earning points. There are even bonus points for eating special stuff. It should be the same thing in your restaurant. Your people should be buzzing around the restaurant, earning as many points as possible.

The more points they earn, the more money they should be paid. You must give the best reward to the people who produce the best results and move the ball forward. You must replace the people who hold you back. The people who always win at Pacman are your Pigs. Pigs love playing Pacman!

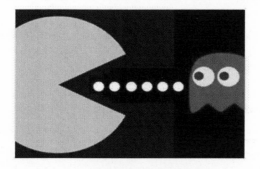

WHO EVER DOES THE MOST WORK MAKES THE MOST $$$

The Reward

You must reward performance that achieves results and moves the ball forward toward the goal. You are either *'for us'* or you are *'against us'*. There is no middle ground. I keep the people who help us move toward the goal and replace the ones who don't. It is either black or white, there is no gray. You are either on time or you are late. A cocktail is either made perfectly, or it is not.

I hate people who say one thing to my face, and go out and do the exact opposite, because they are too spineless to debate the issues on merit and stand up for the team! I am NOT looking for yes men, and women who stroke my ego and agree with my every whim and request. I want people with guts, who are willing to stand up and fight for what they believe.

I do not tolerate turf wars. It's OK to disagree and argue, as long as you are fighting for the best thing for the business, the team, and THE CUSTOMER!

If you are fighting for the cheap way or the easy way, you will be destroyed!

This works both ways, the customers, managers and employees are asking themselves the same question. Is the boss—the leader—for us or against us?

The Schedule

The schedule is one of my absolute favorite topics in the entire world. The schedule is the SINGLE MOST IMPORTANT document in any restaurant.

The schedule determines the fate of every shift and the ultimate success or failure of your restaurant. The schedule is like the starting lineup of a major league baseball team. The team with the *best* players and the *best* schedule always wins.

The schedule matters to you and your people. The schedule is so important that some employees, even take pictures of it. Every employee needs to know two things.

1. How much do I get paid?
2. When do I work?

The schedule tells them when they work and how many hours they will get. When your people look at the schedule, they are calculating the number of hours multiplied by their hourly pay rate. This tells them how much money they will make. This is *very* important to them.

The person who writes the schedule has power over the people on it, and the people on the schedule have power over the person who writes the schedule. This is a two-way street.

When you don't have enough people to fill the schedule, you are at the *mercy* of your people, and you will have to beg them to work extra. You may even have to dole out special favors or privileges just to get them to help you. AND, you will have to put people on the schedule who are under-qualified.

If you have too many people and you schedule them when *they* want to work, your labor cost will out of control, AND you will have too many people on Tuesday when it is slow, and not enough on Saturday when it is busy.

If you are a smart manager, you will schedule the best performers (pigs) first and give the not so good performers (chickens & employees) what is left. This is the best way to do it.

There are two important parts of a great schedule:

1. 100% of the shifts must be filled with *well-trained & talented* people
2. You must have *100% Attendance* for every shift. Yes, *every* shift.

Nothing is more important than the schedule. You must write an effective schedule. You must have talented people at every position.

Here's an important question, pay attention: Do you have the *best* people in your market at every position? If not, why not? The answer to this question is really important. There are three reasons you don't have the best people in your market at every position.

1. You are not willing to pay the price, because you are cheap.
2. The best people will not work for you, because you are a jerk.
3. You are a bad recruiter, because you are lazy.

Think about recruiting as a real important function of your business. Now, take a look at your schedule. Is your schedule filled with the *best* people in your market?

Here is the three-million-dollar question: What will it take to have the *best* team in your market? What will it take to have the *best* waiters, cooks, bartenders and managers? Are you willing to do what it will take to make that happen? Or, are you satisfied with warm bodies?

Do you want the "warm body restaurant" or the BEST restaurant? The answer to that question is written all over your schedule. Don't believe me? Take a look for yourself.

Thinking Exercise

Let's imagine that you have a seasonal business. During the busy time you have 160 hours of work. You have four employees who each work 40 hours per week.

During the slower months, there are only 120 hours of work. What do you do? Do you drop everybody down to 30 hours? Or, do you eliminate one of the people?

Personally, I would eliminate the weakest performer, here's why. If I cut everybody back to only 30 hours, it is a guarantee that I will lose the best player. The reason is because the best player will have no trouble finding a full-time job. This will create a situation where we are left with #2, #3 and #4. Our team will get weaker.

This happens because there is no such thing as a team of four equal people. Yes, this even goes for partners in an LLC. One person always does more than the others and one person always does the least. This is the way the world has and will always work. We will discuss this further in the section about the 20-70-10.

100% Attendance

I believe that missed shifts are the biggest problem in the restaurant industry today. I believe missed shifts are responsible for 80% of all customer complaints—that's right 80%!

This chronic problem is a major cause of employee dissatisfaction and turnover. Missed shifts kill the positive vibe in a restaurant, because everybody knows they will have to work harder to cover them, and it's usually the same few people (shit heads) who call off the most. The missed shifts epidemic needs to be fixed. Now!

I believe that 80% of missed shifts are the direct result of weak management. Weak managers hire the wrong people, write lousy schedules and fail to confront the people who constantly miss work. Most restaurant managers accept the fact that people are going to call off work on a regular basis, and they don't even bother to document the missed shifts when they happen. This happens in restaurants that are managed by chickens or people with self-entitlement syndrome—This is INSANE!

I put missed shifts in two categories:

1. Excusable Absences
2. Un-excusable Absences

Excusable Absences represent 20% of missed shifts. This is when people actually are too sick to come to work, or they have a real personal or family emergency. This includes really weird things such as crazy weather, snow days and floods. These are good reasons to miss work. However; these absences only account for 20% of missed shifts and are not the real problem.

Un-excusable Absences represent 80% of missed shifts. These are un-forced errors (fumbles) that cause havoc on your restaurant, fellow team members and customer service. They come in two categories:

1. Management Error
2. B.S. Excuses from Employees & "Chickens"

Management Error:

- The manager who writes the schedule makes a mistake.
- The schedule gets posted late and people don't know when they are supposed to work.
- The manager only schedules five waiters for the weekend, when we know we need seven.
- The manager fails to add extra people to cover a (known) special event or a spike in business.
- The manager schedules two key people for vacation the same week.
- The manager fails to replace someone on the schedule, who recently quit.

- The manager approves a schedule change but doesn't change the posted schedule.
- The manager makes a schedule change but doesn't tell anyone.
- The manager fails to check requests for days off and gets caught short at the last minute, by one of the chickens.
- The manager continues to schedule employees who constantly miss work.
- The biggest error is not having enough trained team members to cover the required shifts.

B.S. Excuses from Employees & "Chickens"

- Calling in sick to go to a party or social event.
- Last minute call offs because a family member (unexpectedly) came home to visit.
- They forgot their best friend was getting married, two days out.
- Went out of town and can't get back, because their car broke down.
- They have to work their "Other Job" today.
- The bus doesn't run today.
- I have to study for a test.
- I got arrested, I'm in jail. (You know this happens!)
- The list is endless...

The point is 80% of missed shifts are directly related to stupidity. If you set the standard and hold your people accountable for their actions, your missed shifts will reduce drastically. You must draw the line in the sand and stand your ground.

I highly recommend that you keep track of missed shifts and discipline people who miss work. I use a point system, (Late = 1 Point / Missed Shift = 5 Points) when you get 20 points in any 90-day period, you are terminated. *Hasta La Vista!*

Keep these two statements in mind as you build your team:

1. You will only be as successful as your people want you to be.
2. Your level of expectation & acceptance will determine your level of success.

You Will Only Be As Successful As Your People Want You To Be

I love that phrase. Your people will literally make or break your restaurant. The quality of every single aspect of your business will be determined by the people who cook the food, make the drinks, serve the customers and wash the dishes. Your restaurant will only be as good as your worst manager, cook, bartender, waiter and busboy.

Everything that you want to accomplish as a business owner depends on OTHER PEOPLE! You can't open the restaurant without a good people. You can't take a day off without good people to run the business.

You must hire the right people and teach them exactly what to do. You must train, coach and lead them! The key word here is right people. Losers, warm bodies, drunks and potheads with entitlement syndrome will not help you achieve greatness.

You cannot afford to waste your time and precious resources on people who look down on the restaurant business and use us until their "real jobs" come along. You must replace the under performers, with winners who work hard AND move the ball forward.

Level of Expectation/Acceptance

You must define the level of quality and performance that you EXPECT from yourself and your team. You must define the level of quality and performance you are willing to ACCEPT.

A strong leader always sets expectation and acceptance standards up front. A strong leader makes sure that every team member understands the goal and knows exactly what their role is.

I have a reputation for blowing people serious heat when they don't do their job. New people ask our managers about what they have to do to avoid the wrath of the Food Guru. One of my managers put it this way, "Peter doesn't hate everybody. He just hates people who suck, so don't suck!"

I want to make it perfectly clear that I wholeheartedly believe people are our most important asset! People make everything possible, and without the right team members we have nothing! The key word here is the RIGHT team members. Some people (20% of Americans) get it, most people (80%) don't.

I believe anyone can fit in the restaurant business, short, tall, fat, skinny, black, white, male, female, cute, not so cute, gay, or straight; it doesn't matter. What *does* matter is how well you do your job. I measure people based on performance. Performance is King!

As restaurant owners and managers, we are always one person short of a full team and we need the new people to start ASAP.

Here's how the hiring process really works in the restaurant business. A candidate fills out an application. If they "kinda sorta" fit what we are looking for, we give them a shot. If they work out that's great. If not, we replace them as soon as possible. When an employee does a good job, they stay. If they don't do the job, they get replaced.

Options

The quality of our choices and decisions always comes down to the options that we have available at the time. Look at your team, every single one of them are here for the same reason. They were the best option that you had available at the time.

Just because someone was your best option a year ago, doesn't mean that you cannot change players, when a better option comes along. Your people are doing the same thing to you.

The best restaurant owners have the best and most options. The success of your business will always come down to the quality of your options. Here's a great quote that I think about often.

"Never allow someone to be your priority, while allowing yourself to be their option."

\- Mark Twain

Self-Entitlement Syndrome

I believe self-entitlement syndrome is one of the biggest epidemics in America today. Self-entitlement syndrome is ruining more lives than any other disease on earth. Self-entitlement syndrome is rampant, and it is the root of many evils that plague your restaurant.

The truth is the world doesn't owe you or me anything. If we want something, it is up to us to get off our asses and go get it.

Every one of us has this virus to some degree. It is up to you to cure yourself first and then help your people identify it and eliminate it. Self-entitlement syndrome is holding us back from achieving our real potential.

Hire Quick, Fire Quicker

We don't hire our way to success, we really HIRE & FIRE our way to success. The absolute truth is that we take a chance on everybody we hire, and they take a chance on us. There is no such thing as the perfect candidate or employee.

Good managers keep the right people, and bad managers keep them all. Managers keep the wrong people around for too long for two main reasons. The first is they are afraid somebody is going to quit, and they don't want to be short-handed. The second is that they are afraid to admit they made a bad hire. They let their ego get in the way.

The thing to remember is that we can give people opportunity and information; whether they do the job or not, is totally up to them. I say, hire quick, fire quicker.

Think about team building like this. You are the head coach. Your goal is to create a culture of excellence and build a winning team. You will do this by surrounding yourself with the best players & team members you can recruit and hire. Hiring decisions always come down to the options that you have available at the time.

You must dedicate yourself to recruiting winners who love life and have a positive attitude. You must teach your team how to operate the system and perform their job to a very high standard. You must teach common people to get above the clouds where they can achieve uncommon results.

Strong leaders measure, rank, post and reward performance. Then, they promote the people who move the ball forward and replace the people who hold them back. Your legacy will be your ability to improve the lives of the people around you. This is how you build a winning team that thrives for many years.

Four Steps of Training & Delegating

In the One Minute Manager, Kenneth Blanchard taught us the Four Steps of delegating. It is a must read for every manager on Earth. This is my abbreviated version of the four steps of training.

Delegation is about assigning specific tasks and/or responsibilities to a specific person or position. Usually from a manager to an employee or team member. For example, the owner will delegate the management of the kitchen to the chef. The chef will delegate the responsibility for washing dishes to the dishwasher.

Training is divided into four steps. The trainer or manager must go through each of these four steps with EVERY employee, on EVERY task of the job and position. You must cover everything from start to finish. The goal is to teach every employee exactly how to do the job. The employee must accept responsibility for the job and perform the job at level four.

Step One: Show & Tell

This is when you explain the job and walk through every step, in great detail. If a cook has ten menu items that come off their station, you must teach them exactly how to prepare all ten items perfectly. You must explain the, who, what, where, when, why and how for every task.

This should include detailed checklists, recipes and pictures for every item. This is a very important step, because the new person must see HOW each task is supposed to be done. Step one is when you teach them what the STANDARDS are. The goal is for the new person to perform EVERY part of the job to the standard.

Step Two: Observe, Correct & Praise

This is when we let the new person perform the actual task. We watch them do it and make corrections to their techniques until they can do it themselves without help. This step is about positive reinforcement as they learn to perform the task to the standard.

The new employee must prove that they understand the specific tasks and can perform each of them to the standard. You should give them lots of verbal and written praise.

As you are aware, most kitchen tasks such as peeling a carrot, baking a potato, and grilling a steak are fairly easy, the difficulty happens when they have to do multiple things and integrate production with the other team members or positions, at the same time. Most cooks can do well with one table or ticket at a time, but when they get ten tables at the same time, things get complicated.

You must work with your new people to make sure they can handle the heat and maintain the standard, especially when it's busy. When you are satisfied that they can properly prepare each menu item, and perform each task to the standard, they can move on to Step Three.

Step Three: Manage from a Distance

Step three is the first time you can leave the new employee to do the job alone. This means that you go back to your job and check in with the new employee periodically, to see that they are still following your detailed instructions and producing every product and doing every task, to the STANDARD.

At step three, you must check back to see if they are still following your detailed instructions, exactly as you have taught them. If the employee is doing it correctly, Great! If they are doing it wrong, you must step in and correct their behavior immediately.

Think about it like this, the new person proved that they are capable of performing the job to the standard in step two. Now they have altered the task and are *not* performing it to your standard.

There are only three reasons why this should happen.

- They are stupid and can't remember how to do it.
- They are incapable of doing it when it gets busy.
- They have no respect for you and your rules and silly little system, they think you are stupid.

Step Three is when we introduce the verbal and/or written reprimand. If the employee proved that they could do the job to the standard in step two, and now they have changed the system, or violated a rule, it is time for a discussion, verbal reprimand and documentation.

The first reprimand can be verbal. The second reprimand (for the same infraction) must be in writing. When you give someone a written reprimand, they know you are serious. Written feedback is REAL feedback, verbal feedback is just a bunch of noise. When you give someone a verbal reprimand, they think you are picking on them, or just being a micromanager. If one verbal reprimand doesn't fix the problem, you must increase the heat!

We use 60-second evaluations for written warnings, they are like getting a speeding ticket. It tells the employee what they did wrong and what they need to do to fix the problem. Written warnings go in the employee's personnel file, and we also give them a copy to take home and post on their refrigerator.

There will be people who cannot perform the job to your standards. When this happens, you can either go back and repeat the training process from Step One or replace the employee. At Step Two the employee should have proven to you that they were capable of performing the task. If the employee has altered the task or is not doing it to the standard. They must make the corrections to their performance or it's "hasta la vista".

Step Four: Meet the Standard
It's Your Job... Do It!

When the new employee has proven they can perform all the duties related to their new position, and they meet the standard. The job becomes their responsibility. It is now their job, and their responsibility to perform without a babysitter.

The goal is to get every employee to Step Four on every task and manage them as a Level Three. You must constantly inspect what you expect to see that every duty and task that happens in your restaurant meets the standard.

When all of your people are performing at Level Four, you can start to upgrade and make improvements. This is how we grow a restaurant.

When the employee gets to Level Four, they go from an employee to a TEAM MEMBER, and they move from training wage to the full wage for the position. Don't pay them the full wage until they PROVE they can actually do the work. If the employee is being paid the FULL wage for the position and they are underperforming, they need to be replaced.

What if they can't get to level four?

If an employee cannot get to Level Four within a fair amount of time, they need to be replaced by someone who can. You cannot keep underperforming employees. You are not in the babysitting business.

Under-Performers make YOU look weak. Under-Performers are losers, they send the wrong message to the winners who are doing a great job and kicking ass. Building a winning team requires COURAGE!

You can never reduce the pay rate of an under-performer, because their performance will get even worse. It is always best to just fire the under-performer and put everybody out of their misery.

Here's how I think about it. Imagine we have an employee who is performing just below the standard. If there is nobody to replace them, they have a job. The minute a new candidate shows up, I replace the underperforming person. If their performance is a real embarrassment, they have to go immediately.

Learn It, Do It, Own It, Improve It

This is a little different spin on the steps of training and delegation. The chart below has five steps, we all fit at a certain level depending on the subject or enterprise. This chart can be used to measure performance at work, home, finance and health. I like to ask each member of my team where they fit with each aspect of their job and their life.

Let's take a look at how this chart works with a restaurant staff.

1. **Avoid It:** This is the baby-sitting stage when we chase adults and beg them to do their job. I don't know about you, but I am a terrible baby sitter, I usually yell and holler and throw things at the babies! I have no respect for entitled people who expect to be paid to do a half assed job and make me mental.
2. **Learn It:** This is when new people learn how to do the job, it's called on the job training.
3. **Do It:** This is when the team member does the work and meets the standard for the job.
4. **Own It**: Good people take ownership of their life and their job. No excuses. This is Good!
5. **Improve It:** This is when people take ownership, work hard, stay focused and move the ball forward. These people find a way to make things work better than before. I love these people.

If your goal is to improve your restaurant, you must surround yourself with people who have the interest and talent to move the ball forward in all aspects of their life. This simple concept can change your life.

Think about it... if your goal is to improve your restaurant, your people must be willing and able to move the ball forward. Your restaurant cannot improve until your people do.

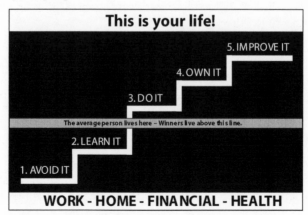

Stair Step Training Program

In Food Guru World we hire *good people* who fit the *culture* and teach them the skills they need to perform the job. We offer every employee the opportunity to grow and move up. Stair step training is the best way I have found to train and grow our own talent.

Several years ago, I needed to hire a new grill cook, to cook 200+ steaks a night. I realized that there was no one qualified in my kitchen, and that if I hired someone from the outside it would take months to get them up to speed with our quality, system and *culture*. This started me on the path to the Stair Step Training System.

Stair Step Training works just like school, people move up from first grade, to second, third and so on. In Stair Step Training, people start in the easiest position and as they learn and grow, they move to the next step. This allows us to "grow" our own players.

We hire two types of people in our restaurants:

1. Rookies/Winners
2. Veterans/The B Draft/Mercenaries

Rookies/Winners

People of *good character* and a *great attitude*, who have no prior restaurant experience. Rookies must have something in their background that shows that they are winners. Rookies start at the beginning and work through the stair step training program.

Veterans/The B Draft/Mercenaries

These are people with prior restaurant experience. Cooks or waiters who have talent and can make the starting lineup with a minimum of training. These people must be winners, have good character and be willing to *follow our system* to the letter. These people must also start at the beginning and work their way up through the system. The amount of time they spend in each position will depend on their talent, how fast they learn and the needs of the business at the time.

Start at the Beginning

It's not the bottom, it's the beginning. Everyone must fit within the culture and follow our system. The military starts everyone in boot camp and so do we. If we are going to have a culture of excellence and a solid system, everyone must know how to perform the basic functions and tasks of every part of the system.

I very rarely hire managers from outside the company because, they don't understand our system and our culture. Outsiders always have their own ways of doing things, they always try to change our system to match what they did at their last job. They usually head off in the wrong direction, which creates confusion and lowers our performance.

Veterans must learn how we do things, and then maybe, they will have the talent to help us improve. I start ALL future managers at the beginning and give them the *opportunity* to climb the stairs at their own pace. By the time they get to the management level, they should understand *why* we do things the way we do, and then they are better equipped to help us make *intelligent* improvements to the system.

The second effect of starting veterans and future managers at the beginning is, we get to watch them in a working role as a *doer*, before they get to a management or leadership role.

I would say that 80% of the time, we discover one of two major flaws.

1. They can't perform the basic tasks—they *suck* at the job!
2. They have a serious character flaw.

Everyone must start at the beginning and work through the system. People can go through the system at their own pace. It's all based on talent, knowledge and performance. Stair Step Training Works!

One of the biggest obstacles restaurant operators face is finding people with the combination of character, work ethic and culinary talent to produce products and service to the standards. When we find people who are great cooks, they often have character flaws that make it impossible to keep them on the team. The best way to solve this problem is to grow your own talent from a pool of people who have strong character traits. I have been working this system for many years and it works great. I'd be lying if I told you it works perfectly, but it is much better than anything else I've tried, and it works better every year.

The Path from Dish Washer to General Manager

In our restaurants, every employee starts at the beginning, in the easiest position and works their way up the steps to the position that requires the most knowledge and talent. Our people can go through the steps quickly or slowly depending on their experience and the needs of the restaurant.

Some people make it to the top, most people fail miserably. That's just the way it is in an organization that has very high standards.

There are two paths in our restaurants. The Kitchen Path, and the Service (dining room) Path. Everyone must do the work, spend the time to *pass* the requirements at every step, before moving up to the next step. There are *no* shortcuts.

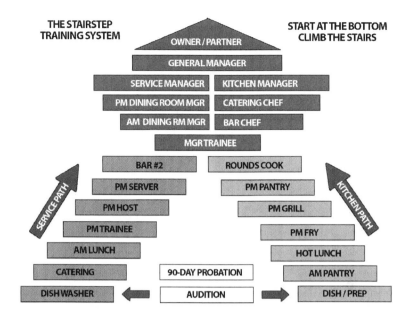

THE STAIRSTEP TRAINING SYSTEM

START AT THE BOTTOM CLIMB THE STAIRS

OWNER / PARTNER

GENERAL MANAGER

SERVICE MANAGER | KITCHEN MANAGER

PM DINING ROOM MGR | CATERING CHEF

AM DINING RM MGR | BAR CHEF

MGR TRAINEE

BAR #2 | ROUNDS COOK

PM SERVER | PM PANTRY

PM HOST | PM GRILL

PM TRAINEE | PM FRY

AM LUNCH | HOT LUNCH

CATERING | 90-DAY PROBATION | AM PANTRY

DISH WASHER | AUDITION | DISH / PREP

SERVICE PATH | KITCHEN PATH

Team Focus

Restaurants are made up of teams and individual players. We have the management team, the sales team, the kitchen team, the service team, the bar team, the office and accounting teams. Each of these teams perform different functions and have slightly different goals.

For example, the goal of the marketing department is to bring customers to the door. The goal of the chef is to produce great food on time. The goal of the Service Manager is to meet the sales goals, deliver the Customer Promise and create satisfied customers, who come back with their friends.

Each manager has multiple goals. The kitchen manager has the goal of a 32% food cost, plus other goals for cleanliness, production and labor cost. The front of the house manager has goals, such as 25% bar cost goal, sales goals and staff training goals.

There are two ways to supersize your team:

1. Get each *team member* headed in the right direction
2. Get each *team* headed in the right direction

It is important for the leader to get the individual people and the individual teams focused and headed in the same direction. In the graphic below we see the typical focus on the left. Most restaurant teams are doing their own thing, and accomplishing their department goals, but they are not in sync.

If you really want your restaurant to thrive, you must get every team and every team member to work together AND head in the same direction. You must teach the individuals and teams to work together, this creates Synergy!

TEAM FOCUS

CURRENT FOCUS   IMPROVED FOCUS

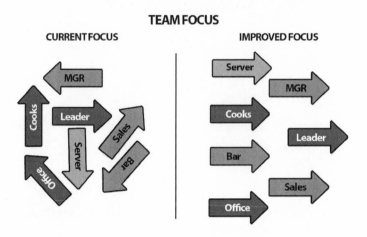

The Team Mindset

Think of a football team. Every team member knows, the team that scores the most points wins. Team members know that, performance counts—the coach is going to put the BEST PLAYERS on the field. If you want to play, you better produce results that move the ball forward and help the team win.

Imagine this scenario. The quarterback takes the snap from center, trips, and drops the ball, what happens? In football, every member of the team dives for the ball, because they know they must recover it before the other team does. A football player will do whatever it takes to recover a fumble and win the game.

When your quarterback (manager) drops the ball, do your people fight for it, or watch it roll around and wait for someone else to save it?

The 20/70/10 Concept

This is a concept that I learned from Jack Welch, in his great book called *Winning*. It is excellent. Here, I will take Jack's concept and adapt it to your restaurant. Here's how it works:

- We *set the standard* for performance at each position.
- We *evaluate & measure* our people based on their performance compared to the standard.
- We *rank* our people based on their performance.

- We *post* the results, so all team members can see how they compare to the rest of the team.
- We *reward* our people based on their performance.
- The *best* performers get the best reward.

When we do this, we find that the results will be divided into what Jack Welch calls the 20/70/10. This is really a twist to the 80/20 theory or Pareto Principle.

- The Top 20% of our people are the Stars, they kick ass, they move the ball forward.
- The Middle 70% do the daily work. We continue to train and encourage these people.
- The Bottom 10% creates problems and need to be replaced.

I want you to think about that for a minute. I'm sure the names of your top 20% instantly popped into your head, because they are the people you can't live without, *and* I'm even more certain that the name of your worst performer also popped into your head.

Now that you know that you have three types of people. Stars, Worker Bees and Problem Children. What are you going to do about it? If you are anything like me, you are going to find ways to reward and keep your stars. Then you are going to find ways to encourage the Middle 70% to keep growing, and then you are going to replace the Bottom 10%.

The secret to building a winning team is to constantly replace the bottom 10% with new people who have the potential to become stars. This one simple concept will change your life, if you have the guts to follow through with it.

I Think of the Top 20% as "A Students". I like to break the middle 70% into two groups. Instead of the middle 70%, I think of it as 35%/35%. The Top 35% are the "B Students". The Bottom 35% are the "C Students". I Think of the Bottom 10% as problem children or enemy combatants. That's right, an enemy combatant is someone who hates what you are trying to do, and fights against you and your goals and dreams. *The enemy combatants must die!*

I want you to imagine this little scenario. You are the leader. You are standing in front of your group. They are all sitting in chairs. The A students are in the front row. The B students in the second row. The C students in the third row and the enemy combatants and problem children are in the back row. You are teaching and coaching your people on how to improve the business, the system and their lives.

Meanwhile, in the back row, the problem children are whispering in the ears of the C students. They are telling the C students how bad this place sucks and how full of crap you are. The poor little C students are conflicted. They don't know which way to turn. Should they listen to you, or should they listen to the losers in the back row. *You know exactly what I'm talking about, don't you...and it drives you crazy, right?*

Your Restaurant's Score

Now, I want you to imagine a different scenario. Imagine that we have 10 people on our team, and we rank them on a scale of 1-10. The best performer is a 10 and the worst performer is a 1.

Let's say our ten people stack up as follows. We have a 10, a 9, an 8, a 7, a 6, a 5, a 4, a 3, a 2, and a 1. When we up these ten scores, we get 55. So, on a scale of 1-10 our team average is a 5.5.

Now, let's imagine that we terminate our worst player (the 1) and replace them with a new person who can play at the 8 level. This will change our score and give us a 10, a 9, two 8's, a 7, a 6, a 5, a 4, a 3 and a 2. Our 1 is gone and replaced by an 8, which is a 7-point improvement. When we add the 7 points to our 55, we increase to 62. This will change our average score from 5.5 to 6.2... not bad for one move.

When we do this again, we replace our next weakest player (the 2) with another 8. Our score will go up by another 6 points. Now we are at a 6.8.

Remember if our goal is to build a winning team of A and B Students who can perform at level 8 or above. We can only hire people who have the potential to perform at Level 8. This means we can't hire losers, whiners, complainers, drunks or potheads. We must hire SMART people who believe in our mission and have a strong desire to WIN!

The key is to replace the under-performers with new players who can score at least an 8. As you replace the people at the bottom of your organization, other people (the C students) may get the hint and start to do better. Some of your C students might improve and become B students. Especially after you kill the enemy combatants and problem children in the back row, who are constantly talking crap and dragging everybody down.

If you stay at this long enough, you will eventually replace the 3, the 4, the 5, the 6, and the 7 with 8's, and your new team will be made up of a 10, a 9, and *eight* 8's which adds up to 83 and your new team average will be an 8.3.

This is how you build a winning team. Good Leaders set the goals and the standards. The team members either achieve the goals or NOT. The choice is totally up to them. You are simply the coach, and they are the players. If they refuse to come up to the standards, it is your DUTY to replace them with new people who can perform to the standards and find ways to improve.

The first few times you do this, it will be pretty easy to do, because you are most likely pissed at them all the time.

As you continue to replace under-performers, it will get much harder because as your standards improve, some of the people who used to be OK or good will no longer "measure up". This is not ruthless; it's survival. It's your duty to build a team of winners who believe in the mission, and by the way, this goes *double* for managers.

Chapter Recap

The key concepts in this chapter are:

- Why would anyone want to work for you?
- Create & build a culture of excellence.
- Share your company values with your people.
- Recruit like a pro.
- Think like the gm of a professional sports team.
- Play Pac Man.
- Write a great schedule & demand 100% attendance.
- Use the four steps of training & delegating.
- Learn it, do it, own it, improve it.
- Use the Stair-Step Training System.
- Master the 20-70-10.

While the ideas in this section are fresh in your mind. I want you to write your team building goals.

Write the names of your "Stars" here:

Write the names of your weakest players here:

What does your DREAM Team look and act like?

My Team Building Goal is:

Write 10 things you can do now (today) to improve your team:

Fundamental # 4:
Build a Customer-Centered Brand

In this chapter we will discuss four important things:

1. We are in the hospitality business. Hospitality is about making people feel special and important.
2. We are in the relationship business. Your ability to build long term relationships will define your life.
3. Design the Experience you want your customer to have from the time they walk in the door, until they pay the check and leave.
4. Train your people to deliver that experience every day for the next 10 years.

Hospitality

You are in the hospitality business. Your #1 product is hospitality! You are also in the relationship business. Your job is to build long-term relationships with the people that you serve. Over and over, day after day, year after year.

Doesn't that sound like the perfect thing to put on a brochure or say to your employees and customers? The funny thing is that most restaurant and hotel owners think that everybody knows how to deliver hospitality. Most people talk about it and hope it happens, but most people never "live" it.

The words "hospitality industry" are a total joke. When someone says, they work in the hospitality industry, that is usually code for, "I can't work at the hospital, because they drug test", or "I am an undereducated loser who hasn't quite found my path, so I will get a job in a restaurant and make some quick bucks, so I can move out of my mom's basement."

What about the service industry? There are some people who refer to our industry as the "service industry". There is even an organization called the

SEIU, (Service Employee International Union). The SEIU is dedicated to creating fairness for (and exploiting) their members, it has nothing to do with improving customer service.

Please allow me to be the first to tell you that 95% of all restaurants and hotels—SUCK at Hospitality—and 95% of all the people who work in the "hospitality industry" and "service industry" SUCK at hospitality.

If that is a little harsh for you, please take a minute to go find a tissue, and come back when you are ready to face reality.

OK, OK, let's back up and start over. I just wanted to get your attention and freak out some of the "sensitive" folks who live in a dream world, where everything is perfect.

Service & Hospitality.

Service is bringing someone a burger or a beer. The Dominos dude who brings a pizza to your house is providing a service, hospitality is optional. Here's my definition of hospitality:

"Hospitality is making people feel special & important."

That is a pretty simple description. Now, let's take it one step further. There are three levels of interaction that you can have with our customers:

1. Transaction
2. Service
3. Relationship

Transaction. Selling the Customer a product. This is the lowest form of selling to a customer. We see this at fast food restaurants and convenience stores. We trade our money for a burger and fries, or a roller dog.

Service. Bringing the Customer a burger or a beer. This is the second level of selling the customer. Service is about doing some of the work, so the customer doesn't have to. We see this in full-service restaurants and with delivery from places like Pizza Hut and Grub Hub.

Relationship. This is when we know the customer by name, and they know us. We know what the customer drinks and which table is their favorite. We say hi to them when we see them around town. We like them, and they like us. It's easy to take great care of these folks, because we have a great relationship!

Above and beyond the three transaction levels is a thing we call—Love & Hospitality! As we have discussed, hospitality is about making the customer feel special and important. Hospitality can happen at any one of the interaction levels—transaction, service or relationship. Hospitality is not about the quality or level of service. It is about love and respect.

Think about the quintessential grandmother, she loves you unconditionally, she can't wait to see you and she will do anything to please you. Think about the one person in your life who exemplifies hospitality, the person who sets the gold standard for love, service and hospitality, and you will know what I am talking about.

The best way to build a culture of hospitality is to hire people who already have the hospitality gene because that is who they are--not who they have to be to get and keep this job. Think about that for a second, it's a really important point.

Fun with Dick and Jane

Here's a fun thing: Every restaurant has a few customers who love the staff. Everyone knows who they are. They bring the staff gifts, they are awesome human beings, and they are great tippers. Some restaurants even invite these special customers to their employee Christmas party.

It is very easy to love and deliver real hospitality to these people because— THEY love you and your staff. Let's call these people Dick and Jane.

What about all your other customers, who are not as famous and outgoing as Dick and Jane? What would happen if every member of your team started treating all your customers like they do Dick & Jane?

I'll tell you what will happen... Your restaurant will be packed, and you will make a lot of money!

From this moment forward—your job, and the job or every person on your team is to deliver love and hospitality to every customer who visits your restaurant. Think of Every. Single. Customer... as Dick & Jane.

The goal of this book is to help you create a great dining experience for EVERY customer. You are here to make every customer feel special and important. You must fall in love with the customer. When you fall in love with your customers—they will fall in love with you, your people, and your restaurant! Every interaction with your customers must convey GENUINE HOSPITALITY.

Hospitality from A Dog

You can learn Hospitality from a dog. This is my dog, Toots. Everybody loves Toots. Do you know why? Because Toots LOVES everybody!

"The Love You Make"

Now Hear This:

- When you *put up* with your customers, they will *put up* with you.
- When you *like* your customers, they will *like* you.
- When you *love & respect* them, they will *love & respect* you.

When your customers love and respect you, they will reward you with their loyalty and boat loads of CASH! Yes, this is personal. Very personal.

If your business is slow, it's because your customers don't like you. The reason they don't like you is because YOU don't like THEM! Put that in your pipe and smoke it.

Your customers are at the tables in the dining room. Your managers are in the office doing useless paperwork. Your cooks are out back smoking cigarettes. Your waiters are in the side station, texting their friends. Who has time for service? Who has time for hospitality? It's time to make a few changes. It's time to get serious about hospitality.

Value = 100% + 1%

Here's a different spin on the WOW Experience that I call the 100% +1%. "Value" happens when you delight the customer by delivering a little more than they were expecting. Value happens when you do your job 100% and then add a little extra something that makes the dining experience special and memorable.

Think about the old-time baker who added an extra donut to the bag of their favorite customers. This idea became known as a baker's dozen. This may seem like a silly thing to you, but it is a real big deal. The idea was NOT "buy 12 and get one donut free". No sir, the extra donut was a little something extra, because the baker loved you. Do you understand the difference?

The Cajun's call it a "lagniappe" when someone gives us a little something extra. You don't have to do it, but it becomes something really special that you can physically feel, when it is done out of love and generosity, not need.

When we create a dining experience that exceeds what the customers can get anywhere else in the market, we win big. The goal is to create a win, win, win situation, where everybody is happy. The customer is happy because they got a lagniappe, the waiter is happy because they got a little extra tip and the owner is happy, because the restaurant is packed with customer advocates.

It is our duty to find small ways to innovate and improve the customer experience by doing 100% + 1% every day for the next ten years. Not because we have to, but because we GET to. In Food Guru World we call this the WOW! Experience. We are always looking for small ways to make the customer say "Wow!" And, it doesn't have to cost money. It can simply be a little extra attention or a small gesture that says, "I care about you."

Here's what happens when you use the 100% + 1 technique. The customer will fall in love with you and your business. They will introduce you to their friends. They will go out of their way to find ways to do business with you. We all want to hang around people who love and care about us. This is human nature. When we go 1% further than we have to, people LOVE it!

I have a sign in my restaurants that reads:

We are here to create a "WOW Experience" for each and every customer we serve. We will accomplish this by exceeding the expectation of our customers.

Making Our Customers Feel Special
Serving Excellent Food
Serving Excellent Drinks
Providing Excellent Service
Going Above And Beyond The Expected
Delivering The Unexpected
Creating Special & Memorable Dining Experiences

Design & Define the Customer Experience

The goal of a business is to create and satisfy the customer. Therefore, creating and satisfying the customer must be the goal of your restaurant. You must know who you are, before you can define your customer experience.

- Visualize the exact experience you want your customers to have.
- Document the experience in great detail.
- Share this vision with your managers and team members.
- Create detailed training materials & checklists for your people.
- Train your people to deliver the experience consistently.

The first step of building a great restaurant is to document what you want the customer to experience. Imagine, writing a screenplay that will open on Broadway and run every night for ten years. I'm talking about the exact experience you want the customer to have, from the time they get out of their car, until they pay the check and leave.

This includes everything from curb appeal, restaurant decor, lighting, hostess welcome, waiters greeting, menu style, food and beverage presentation, service standards, restrooms cleanliness, staff interaction, manager interaction, ground game marketing, payment of the check, to the host saying, thank you and inviting them to return.

The dining experience of a burger joint, a sushi bar and a white tablecloth restaurant will be very different. The more detail you use to describe the experience you want your customer to have, the better. You cannot leave this to chance and allow your employees to make it up as they go.

You must teach and lead your people to create a consistently excellent experience. Some highlights for your description should include:

- Type of Restaurant: Fast food, Quick Serve, Steak House, Italian
- Location, ambiance, décor, music, TV selections
- Price Point: High-end or discount pizza joint
- Menu Selections: Made from scratch or heat and serve
- Service Standards: Self-serve, casual, full serve, or fine dining

Document the exact experience and teach every manager and team member to perform their role:

- Your employees are the actors in your play.
- You must create exact job description & scripts for your people.
- You must train every actor to deliver the perfect performance!
- You must cast the right people for each and every part.

For example: A 16-year-old zit-faced kid would not be believable as a wine sommelier in a four-star restaurant, but he might be perfect in a burger joint.

We are not trying to build robots. We are trying to create a consistently excellent dining experience. Think about an iPhone, they are perfectly designed and manufactured to exact standards. How about your products, are they consistent and exact? Or are they all over the map?

Burger Joint Example

I am going to use a simple burger joint with three menu items to illustrate my point. Imagine a restaurant that serves only three things.

1. Cheeseburger
2. Fries
3. Coke

(Ok, we will add Sprite and bottled water.)

The goal is to make the World's Best Cheeseburger. Everything we do must support the burger. We will grind fresh beef chuck throughout the day as needed to fill demand. We will cook each burger to order on a flat top griddle. We will top each burger with Swiss and American cheese.

The buns will be made in house and baked hourly, so the place smells amazing. We will toast each bun and put spicy mayo and house-made dill pickles on them. The burgers may be ordered as a single, double, or triple.

We will not use lettuce or tomatoes on our burgers, because the quality will vary too much from season to season. Our fries will be cut and fried to order, one size only, large. We will salt the fries and serve them with ketchup. Coke, Sprite and water will be served in 20-ounce bottles.

In the example above, we know exactly who and what we are, and we know exactly who we are not. We have a simple understandable goal: Make the World's Best Cheeseburger. Think how simple it would be to operate this restaurant. When we know our goal, every team member can go for it with all their heart and not allow anything to get in the way of the quest to make the World's Best Cheeseburger.

Dealing with Deviations

Let's imagine that a vegetarian comes in to our restaurant and asks for a black bean burger and a salad. What do we do? We say sorry, but we are a cheeseburger joint. We do not have to apologize or try to change who we are. We simply cannot accommodate this person.

Plumbers don't clean windows and we don't sell vegetarian food. We also don't do milkshakes, because they will bring in too many variables that will distract us from our mission: serving the World's Best Cheeseburger.

When we know exactly what our product is, we can describe what happens from the time the customer walks in the door until they leave. We describe the ambiance, the signage, the prices, the service.

We describe the staff, and their uniforms. We describe every step of the experience, just like producing a movie, we write the script, design the costumes, design the set and hire the actors.

Consider Your Restaurant

Think about your restaurant. Does everything you do support and enhance your core product and concept?

The goal is for your restaurant to run exactly the same as it has been designed to run, day after day, just like re-watching your favorite movie. Anything that distracts from or does not support your core concept is "grunge", and grunge must be eliminated.

Here are a few questions to ask yourself:

- What is the story you are trying to tell?
- Exactly what do you want your customer to perceive?
- Does everything you are doing add to that description?
- Does everything support the story you are trying to tell?

Over time, your story or concept can and should evolve and improve, but you must never abandon your core concept. It's OK to improve the quality of your ingredients, but never add a "veggie burger" because that will take your focus off of what makes you and your restaurant, who you are!

It's smart to improve your systems and make things run smoother, but it's stupid to let your people start taking short-cuts because it's easier.

When you know exactly what you want your customer to experience, you can turn that message into... "The Customer Promise".

The Food Guru's Customer Promise

The Customer Promise is what we promise to do for every customer we serve. This is my Customer Promise. I hang in in the kitchen of every restaurant I manage:

- Clean, safe, comfortable place
- Clean plates, glasses and flatware
- Good food and drink at a fair price
- Hot food hot—cold food cold
- Build rapport with the customer
- Make the customer feel special

79

- Deliver first class hospitality
- Give professional, knowledgeable, attentive, prompt service
- Give the customer a little something extra (100% +1)
- Encourage the customer to have fun
- Give your best service, smile, attitude
- Anticipate the customer's needs
- Offer the customer our best food and drink options
- Present the correct bill for services rendered
- Handle financial transaction efficiently
- Thank the customer sincerely
- Give the customer a good reason to return
- If you make a mistake, apologize and correct it immediately

When was the last time that you went to a restaurant, and they hit every one of these points? The goal is to deliver the Customer Promise at every table, every night for the next ten years. When you deliver every point on this list, your customers will say, "Wow!"

Three Key Elements

Think of your restaurant as a brand made up of these key elements:

1. Your People
2. Your Customers
3. Your Products
4. Your Physical Building & Ambiance

This includes everything the customer sees, hears, feels, and smells during a dining experience.

Think of your customer as a super-sophisticated being who enters your restaurant and evaluates everything and everyone they come in contact with. The customer will evaluate how they are treated, the environment around them and the product that you serve them. If any of these elements are less than what the customer expects, you will lose. If these elements meet or exceed the customer's desires, you win!

Build a "Cult Following"

Your marketing must support your concept and your brand. Your marketing must teach your employees and customers exactly who you are, what you do, and why that is important to them.

Your employees must support your concept and your brand. When your employees love your brand, they become brand ambassadors. When your customers love your brand, they also become brand ambassadors.

Think of a brand like In & Out Burger. They have a cult following of raving fans who love and support their brand. Imagine what would happen if they hired employees who did not eat meat?

It's the same thing in your restaurant. You must hire people who love your brand and are members of your cult. People who are in love with the product, have the ability to infect others with their enthusiasm and help you build a cult.

Smart restaurant operators have a very narrow focus. They know exactly who they are, and they surround themselves with people who also love what they are doing. Smart restaurant operators know exactly:

1. Who they are
2. Where they are going
3. Who they want to bring along for the ride

When you create a great brand, and you are true to your brand, like-minded people will flock to you. Be Brave, Be True to Your Brand, Be Cult-Worthy.

Chapter Recap

The key concepts in this chapter are:

- Hospitality = Making People Feel Special & Important
- Value = 100% +1%
- Customer Experience: Write the screenplay for your restaurant
- The Wow Experience
- Define Your Customer Promise & Share it With Your People
- Sell Your Core Product to Your Core Audience
- Build a Cult Following

While the ideas in this section are fresh in your mind, I want you to detail exactly what you want the customer to experience when they visit your restaurant.

1. What is the number one thing that my restaurant stands for?
2. What is the MOST IMPORTANT thing I want the customer to remember about my restaurant?
3. Write 10 things you want the customer to experience when they visit your restaurant.
4. Get together with your staff and define your vision for what you want your restaurant to be.
5. Create a map or document that details the customer experience from the time they enter your restaurant, until they pay the bill and leave. This exercise will help you get your entire team on the same page and improve the customer experience.

Make a list of 10 Things you can do to improve the Customer Experience.

Fundamental #5:
Build a Marketing & Sales System

Sales are the lifeblood of your restaurant. Sales determine if and when you pay your bills. Sales determine how much you can pay your people. Sales determine how much you can pay yourself. Sales make the wheels turn, without sales, your restaurant is dead.

The amount of sales in your restaurant will determine the quality of your life from the neighborhood you live in, to where your kids go to school and where (or if) you get to take your family on vacation.

In this short chapter, I will lead you step by step through some simple techniques that you can use to get *two 10% sales increases in the next 90-days.*

Six Ways to Increase Sales

In all the World there are only Six ways to increase sales, here they are, with a quick overview.

1. Keep the Customers You Have
2. Bring In New Customers
3. Increase the Average Check
4. Increase Customer Visits
5. "86" the Wrong Customers
6. Raise Your Prices

#1 — Keep the Customers You Have

You do this by delivering on the Customer Promise. The Customer Promise is what you promise to do for your customer in exchange for their money. If you say you have the best cheeseburgers in the world, your cheeseburgers better be pretty damn good.

To keep your customers, you must focus on your core concept. Your product must be aimed at your target audience and delivered to them in a consistently excellent way, every time they visit. You cannot afford to get distracted. You must stay focused on your core product and your target customer.

Your customers react to the way you treat them. If you like them, and give them respect, they will like and respect you, too. If they like you, they will return. If they don't like you, they will not return, it really is that simple.

Losing customers is called—Attrition. Attrition is the gradual reduction of customers. When you just go through the motions and treat your customers with indifference, they will leave you and go to someone else, who likes them better. Yes, this is personal, *very* personal.

80% of your future sales will come from your existing customers, the people in your dining room right now. The secret ingredient in keeping the customers you have is HOSPITALITY. I invite you to get out of the office and go show your employees and customers what first-class hospitality looks like.

#2 — Bring in New Customers

The job of marketing is to bring in new customers. Bringing in new customers will help you counter attrition and GROW!

There are two ways to bring in new customers:

1. Hook them with your marketing and advertising.
2. Have your customers hook them for you, with positive word-of-mouth references.

Word-of-mouth is also called "referral marketing". When your customers return and bring their friends with them, that is the best form of marketing on the planet.

#3 — Increase the Average Check

Sell more to each customer. You will increase the average check, by selling an extra drink, bottle of wine, appetizer or dessert. We call this Upselling. In the restaurant, Upselling is done at the table by waiters with "sales skills".

Imagine, what would happen to your business, if you increased your average check by 10%. What would it take to increase your average check? How many different ways can you think of to increase your average check? In a few minutes, I'm going to show you how to get every four-top in your restaurant, to spend like a five top.

#4 — Increase Customer Visits

The goal is to make a positive impact on your customers and get them to return more often. This will happen when you give them a good reason to return, such as:

- They like you because you and your people make them feel special and important.
- You give them great value for their money.
- They like your food, drinks and/or ambiance.
- You are in a convenient location for them.

Do you know who your customers are? Or are they just faces who come and go? Do you know the names of your core customers? Do you say "Hi" to them when you see them around town? Could you imagine if your doctor, lawyer or grocery supplier didn't know your name, address, or phone number, how would that make you feel?

Remember, 80% of your future sales will come from your current customers. Keeping all the customers you have right now is the most important part of your sales engine. The best way to increase customer visits and get them to return more often, is to take care of them, respect them, know who they are and keep in touch with them.

#5 — "86" The Wrong Customers

This one is a little tricky, so pay please attention. The objective is to sell your goods and services to your target market. The people who understand and appreciate your core concept. It also means that you should focus your marketing efforts on attracting your "target customer".

If you want to be the best cheeseburger joint in America, you need to create a world class burger experience for people who love cheeseburgers, the cheeseburger aficionados, meat eaters and carnivores. Think back to our Cheese Burger Joint example, we want to sell a cheeseburger, fries and a Coke, everything else is "grunge". Grunge takes us away from our core purpose of making the World's Greatest Cheeseburger! Well, it's the same thing in your restaurant, no matter what your concept is.

In the cheeseburger scenario, the wrong customer is a vegan, who wants you to put a black bean burger on the menu, so they can fit in and eat there, too. The wrong customer wants you to abandon your mission just to please them.

Don't be fooled, these are the wrong customers! You must have the guts to stick to your core concept and tell the vegan, "No!" I guarantee that they will be insulted; that's just life, but your REAL customers will get to keep their awesome cheeseburger, and your restaurant will become famous.

By the way... I called around, and I can't find a single vegan restaurant that serves corn-fed beef.

#6 — Raise Prices

You are NOT Walmart. You are NOT in the discount business. Your prices must be fair to the customer and the owner. If you charge too much, your customers will go where they can find better value. If you don't charge enough you will go out of business. Now that you understand the Six Ways to Increase Sales, let's move on to the next step.

Two 10% Sales Increases

My goal is to start a restaurant revolution. I want you to increase sales by 10% TWICE in the next 90 days. I am going to show you exactly how to do it, right now.

If you follow these simple instructions, you will see TWO 10% SALES INCREASES in the next 90-days. But you have to do exactly what I'm going to tell you to do. Anything short of 100% effort will make you fall short. This idea has worked for me over and over again in many different types of restaurants.

This is a four-step process:

1. RAISE PRICES by 10% Today, don't be scared, just do it!
2. Increase Your Customer Count by 5% = MARKETING.
3. Increase Your Average Check by 5% = SALES.
4. Improve Your Performance by 1% Every Day = EFFORT.

My mission is to liberate every hard-working restaurant owner from the fear of closing the doors and losing their business. I want you to take the bull by the horns and start living the life of your dreams. I want you to move way beyond struggling for survival. I want you to THRIVE!

80% of restaurant owners work their asses off just to break even at the end of the year—there is a better way. I believe that 80% of Independent Restaurants are under-charging for their goods and services, and only 20% are charging an amount that is fair to both the owner and the customer. It is time for 80% of the restaurants in America to raise prices! Yes, We Can! Yes, You Can!

Grocery prices went up by 14% in the last two years. Your employees are demanding higher wages and benefits—what about YOU? Don't you want a raise?

Employee strikes and walkouts are all over the news. The SIEU (Service Industry Employee Union) is demanding $15 and hour minimum and health care for all workers. I say, "Let's give it to them." The best restaurateurs charge top dollar and pay their people great wages. It's time for you to do the same.

Raise Prices Now

Raise your prices by 10%, today. Then work your ass off to improve everything you do. This simple move will increase your sales by 10%. You can do this TODAY, without spending an additional dime on food, beverage, labor, overhead or advertising.

If you are serious and really want to or need to increase sales overnight, raising prices is the best and fastest way to do it. Most of your customers have no idea what your prices are and will gladly pay a few more dollars for an excellent dining experience.

Prices need to be fair to both the customer and the owner. You are not Walmart. It is time to get out of the discount game. You cannot charge quick serve prices in a full-service restaurant!

Think about it… Who told you to set your prices where they are? Is anyone holding you back or stopping you from raising prices? What are you really waiting for? I believe you may be afraid to increase your prices because of the following reasons:

- People are hurting from the recession. (The only recession is in your mind.)
- Your food & services aren't worth your current prices. (80% believe this.)
- You are not willing to do the hard work to improve your quality and service. (Are you?)
- Resistance from partners, managers, employees, family, and yourself. (Time to step up.)
- You can't visualize yourself as financially successful. (I Can!)

What is the worst thing that could happen if you raise prices? If some of your customers get upset and go somewhere else, that's OK. Here's why…

The first people who will leave you, only come to your restaurant because it's cheap or you gave them a deal or a coupon. If your customers leave you because of a dollar or two, your problem is much bigger than price.

The second group who might leave you are the whiners and complainers. Whiners and complainers want to keep you and your team focused on price and problems. I say, "let the whiners go next door and drive your competitor crazy!" You need to develop a positive attitude and focus on the good, not the bad. It's time to get and stay positive!

What are you really afraid of? I'll tell you what you are afraid of—it's called success. It's true, most people live in the shallow end of the pool and simply can't imagine themselves being rich and successful. 80% of Americans sabotage themselves every time they start to win. Are you doing this?

The second thing you could be afraid of is, when you raise prices, you will also have to raise the quality of everything you do. That, my friend, is my point. I want you to improve the quality of everything you do!

I say, call the printer and raise prices—today. Why bother struggling through life when you can thrive. It is silly to keep yourself in financial bondage when you can simply raise your prices by a mere 10%. Your restaurant must make a profit, or you will be forced to close. I had to close a restaurant back in 2009. I know first-hand, how bad it hurts! You must do whatever it takes to stay alive.

There is a better way. Your objective is to focus on delivering an excellent customer experience. If your only marketable position is low price, you are in big trouble. The goal is not to survive; the goal is to *thrive*.

"The significant problems we have cannot be solved at the same level of thinking with which we created them."

- Albert Einstein

I love that quote. It means that we must rise above our small thinking and start to THINK BIG. We must look for bigger, better and smarter solutions that release us from the mental bondage of the past. When we think big, we break our mental chains and move forward toward success. When we think small, we stay locked in fear. Fear creates stress, stress makes it impossible to see the simple solutions that are right in front of us. *Stress makes us Stupid!*

Stress Makes Us Stupid!

After you have raised prices, you can use the ideas you learn from this book to ADD VALUE to the customer experience. It is your THINKING that has created the problems that are holding you back from realizing your dreams.

You have a choice: You can stay the victim of the circumstances (which you created), or you can learn from your mistakes, and mine, and build a winning plan for success.

Think about this. What do you expect to pay for a pizza delivered to your house? I would expect to pay between $10 and $20, which means the market expects a range from $10-$20. If that is true, why would you ever want to sell a pizza for $11 or $12?

If your pizza uses premium ingredients and you have a high degree of service, you must charge more than the guy across the street who uses commodity ingredients and has no servers.

The low-price model doesn't make sense... it is a race to the bottom.

You are not in the discount business, or the coupon business. When was the last time YOU, personally, brought a coupon to a restaurant? Quit giving stuff away! You must have the guts to charge full price. You must create a product that is so good your customers will pay full price for it. Your prices must be fair to the customer AND the owner! This is a really big deal... it's time to stop screwing yourself.

Stop the Race to the Bottom. Many restaurant owners think the only way they can compete is with low prices. I say the best way to compete is by delivering an excellent dining experience time after time. It doesn't matter if you are a burger joint or a white table restaurant. You should be focused on what you are GREAT at and have the guts to charge FULL Price!

"Quality is remembered, long after the price is forgotten."

     - Aldo Gucci

The Effect of the 10% Price Increase

In the example below, under the current prices, we see a restaurant with $750,000 in sales, that is breaking even. In the second column, we see that the 10% price increase makes our sales $825,000.

When we raise prices by 10% our sales increase by $75,000. This $75,000 increase will go straight to the bottom line as profit. The only thing that will change is the TOP LINE SALES.

We will not need to bring in any extra customers or sell any additional food or drinks, therefore it will not require any extra food, bar stock or labor expense. The only additional expense will be for printing menus and credit card fees.

- The Cost of Goods will stay the same, $250,000.
- The Labor Cost will stay the same, $250,000.
- Other Cost will stay the same, $250,000.

This will change the Profit from making $0 to making $75,000 in one simple move! This price increase will also lower the cost percentages:

- Cost of Goods will go from 33.3% to 30.3%
- Labor Cost will go from 33.3% to 30.3%
- Other Costs will go from 33.3% to 30.3%
- Profit will move to 9.1%

	Current Prices		10% Price Increase	
Sales	$750,000		$825,000	
Cost of Goods	$250,000	33.30%	$250,000	30.3%
Labor Costs	$250,000	33.30%	$250,000	30.3%
Other Costs	$250,000	33.30%	$250,000	30.3%
Total Expenses	$750,000	100%	$750,000	90.9%
Profit/Loss	$0	0.0%	$75,000	9.1%

And now for the fun part! As you begin to integrate the Eight Basic Fundamentals, your performance will improve, and your sales will naturally increase by another 10%. When this happens, your numbers will look like the third category in the chart below… WOW!

	Current Prices		10% Price Increase		10% Price Increase	
Sales	$750,000		$825,000		$907,000	
Cost of Goods	$250,000	33.30%	$250,000	30.3%	$272,000	33.0%
Labor Costs	$250,000	33.30%	$250,000	30.3%	$250,000	30.3%
Other Costs	$250,000	33.30%	$250,000	30.3%	$250,000	30.3%
Total Expenses	$750,000	100%	$750,000	90.9%	$772,000	85.1%
Profit/Loss	$0	0.0%	$75,000	9.1%	$135,000	14.9%

These TWO 10% Sales Increases have changed the profit in our example from ZERO to $135,000. This is a HUGE improvement on the bottom line. This can literally happen in your restaurant in the next 90-Days if you commit to improving quality and adding value to every part of your business.

One of my restaurants used this simple system and their sales went from $840,000 to $1,040,000 in the first year. Last year, that restaurant did over $1,700,000. The second restaurant I did this with, saw a 40% sales increase in the first year, a 25% the second year and has more than doubled sales since we started the process. This can happen to your restaurant when you get serious.

Let's See Your Numbers

I want you to take out your P&L Statement and write your current numbers in a format similar to the one above. It is important for you to see where you are today, so you can use it as a baseline for the huge improvement that is headed your way.

1. Plug in your Sales, Cost of Goods, Labor Cost & Other Cost.
2. Then, add your Cost together to get your Total Expense.
3. Then subtract your Total Expenses from Sales, to get your Profit.
4. Then calculate the percentages for each category and plug it in.
5. This is simply your starting point to use as a reference going forward.

Then, make a second box. In this second box I want you to increase your sales by 10%. Because we are only increasing prices, you will not have any additional expenses. So, leave all the other numbers the same as Box #1. Then calculate and plug in your new percentages.

I'll bet you will like these potential numbers a lot more than your current numbers. Let's keep going to see what will happen when we get the second 10% sales increase.

In a third box, increase your sales by an *additional* 10%. This time I want you to take the cost of goods percentage from Box #2 and multiply it times sales to get your cost of goods for this example. Then, leave Labor and Other Cost the same as Box #1 & #2.

These potential numbers can happen in your restaurant as soon as you're ready. The choice is up to you: Raise prices, improve quality, add value and thrive, OR do nothing and continue to struggle.

Three Areas of Marketing

In your restaurant, marketing takes place in three areas:

1. The Market
2. The Message
3. The Media

The Market

Do you know who your target customer is? Do you know what they want? Think about what you sell and the person who wants to buy it... that's your market. Your market is your target customer. The people who want or need to buy your product. Your market is the people who you had in mind when you designed and built your restaurant.

Your marketing must match the type of restaurant that you are AND it must appeal to your target audience. All you have to do is talk to the people who make up your market.

If you are a burger joint, you talk to burger lovers. If you are a seafood restaurant, you go after the fish lovers. If you are a vegan restaurant, you go after vegans. *This sounds simple, because it is... don't over think marketing, keep it simple.*

Be #1 or #2 In Your Market

This is a BIG Point. There are many different styles and types of restaurants from breakfast places to burger joints, taco joints and steak houses. Your restaurant must be the #1 or #2 restaurant in your category. If you are the #7 taco joint in town, you will die.

You must work to get to the top two spots. If you cannot get to the top of your category, you should either get out of the business or switch to another category that you can become #1 or #2 in.

Once you identify and develop your concept, you must be able to tell a potential customer who you are and why you are the BEST choice for them in 30 seconds or less. Your newest employee must be able to define your concept and tell a potential customer why you are the BEST choice for them, in 30 seconds or less!

Imagine, that a reporter from the local TV station walks into your restaurant, and sticks a camera in your face and says, we are doing a spot for the 6:00 news, please tell our viewers why they should dine in your restaurant.

You have 30 seconds to explain... ready, go! Are you prepared? Now, imagine that your newest waiter is being interviewed, are you scared? Me too! You get the point, right? Great marketing gets people's attention, but not just any people... YOUR people in YOUR market.

The Message

Marketing is storytelling. You simply tell the story about your restaurant. Here's a few questions to think about:

- What makes you special, unique, and different?
- Who are YOU and why should anyone care?
- What type of restaurant do you operate?
- What are you good at?
- What do you specialize in?

Are you really special or are you just about the same as everybody else? Your marketing message must magnify your CORE product to your CORE audience. You must teach your customers WHY your restaurant is the BEST choice for them in the market.

Your Competitive Edge

In an age when most people are following the herd, your differences will allow you to stand out from the crowd and be noticed. The difference between you and your competition is your Competitive Edge. It is also called your USP: Unique Selling Proposition.

Think of your restaurant as a product on a shelf. What is different about your restaurant? What separates you from your competition? Why should a customer choose you over the competition? Here are some examples:

- Breathtaking View
- 100 Wines by the Glass
- The Best Cheeseburger in America
- Best Steak in Town. Corn Fed USDA Prime Black Angus Beef
- Hand-Crafted Cocktails & Fresh-Squeezed Juice
- Great Sushi: We use Alaskan King Crab (not that fake Surimi)

Consistent Message & Systems

Your USP must be the central point of your Customer Promise and Marketing Message. You must build your Restaurant System and your Marketing Plan around your USP. Your restaurant operation and your marketing must be in perfect alignment.

Share the Message

You must share your USP with your staff, you must share your USP with your customers, you must *become* your USP! You must *scream* your USP and your message from the top of the mountain.

Great marketing is telling your customer who you are, what you do and why you are the BEST choice for them. Smart Restaurant Owners focus on their CORE CONCEPT. The goal is to sell your core product to your core audience, everything that you do should support and enhance your core product. Your marketing should line up perfectly with the customer promise and what is happening inside the restaurant.

Tell your unique story and make it real! Does everything you do support the story you are trying to tell? Does your core product, line up with the style of service, ambiance and price structure?

The Big Four Marketing Questions

Here are the Big Four Marketing Questions that your potential customers (target audience) will need the answer to—*before* they come to your restaurant. So, be sure your marketing story answers them. I ask myself these questions every time I consider a new menu item or do any type of marketing.

1. WIIFM – What's in it for me? What do I get?
2. Obvious Benefit – The obvious benefit of your product or service?
3. Dramatic Difference – Between you and everybody else.
4. Reason to Believe – Why should I believe what you say?

Features & Benefits

The answers to these questions will be presented as Features & Benefits. *Features* are things like USDA Prime Beef. Fresh Fish. Farm to Table or Locally Grown. Wine Spectator Award Winning Wine List. Spectacular View. Excellent Service. Features are important, but benefits are more important.

Benefits are what the product or features will do for the customer. The overall benefit could be great times with friends and family. The benefit of a

93

glass of wine or a cocktail is that you catch a little buzz and feel great! The benefit of 40 Wines by the glass is a wide variety, and maybe even a little education.

Features are great, but benefits make the sale. It's important to tie the benefit of your restaurant to something that makes sense for your type of restaurant. If you are a fast food place, your benefit could be speed. If you offer a buffet, your benefit could be speed and variety.

Some benefits are sexy, some are basic, just remember to connect your features and benefits to your style of restaurant. The benefit of food is that it fills our stomach and, it gives us energy (not-sexy). The benefit of organic vegetables is there are no harmful pesticides (not-sexy).

The Media

This is the Air Campaign, sometimes called one-to-many advertising. The purpose is to get customers to your restaurant. Advertising is when you buy an ad from a media company such as a newspaper, magazine, TV or radio station. Then the company distributes your message to their customers or subscribers.

The upside is that you get to speak to their followers. The downside is that you have to fit into their format and pay for the service. This could be good or bad depending on the media outlet you select, your budget, and your message. *Mass Media (TV, radio, newspaper, and print) is the most expensive and least effective way to market.*

Having said that I would recommend that you pick <u>ONE</u> form of mass media/traditional advertising to drive people into your marketing funnel. Pick the one that makes the most sense to you in your market.

Think back to your target customer, the people who are most interested in what you are selling. Ask yourself, what forms of media are they using? Where can I find them? What local magazines or newspapers are they reading? Is there a local TV program that they watch, or a specific radio DJ that they listen to? Every city & town has some form of media that will work for you, you just need to figure out what it is. People want and need to know what is going on around them.

If you are anything like me, there will be one or two media outlets that work for your brand. Call them and speak to a sales representative. Interview the various sales reps and ask them questions like:

- Who is your audience?
- What will my ads look or sound like?
- How much will it cost me to reach the audience?
- Would you be interested in doing a trade? (For example, I *love* trading advertising for gift certificates!)

94

After the interviews, you should have a clear favorite. I recommend that you start with only ONE form of media. The trick in media advertising is figuring out if it is working or not. How will you measure if your new business is coming from the new advertising or your social media marketing?

You could create a special promotion for people who hear or read your ad. Maybe you could create a comment card that asks new customers how they heard about you?

I like to think of advertising as an investment. If I invest $1,000, how much did I get back? This gets really complicated, because of repeat business after the initial sale. Which brings us back to the ground game. When your Ground Game and Social Marketing reach critical mass, you should be able to pull back on traditional marketing and save some serious cash.

Public Relations (PR)

Another way to spread your message is through the use of Public Relations. This is when we create a press release and send it to media outlets, newspapers, magazines, TV and radio stations. Then, if the media company deems your message worthy, they may call you for more details and possibly run a story about you or your restaurant. The difference between Advertising and PR is that we buy advertising, but we earn PR.

I want to spend a few minutes discussing PR, so pay attention.

Public relations is about managing the public's perception (good or bad) of you and your restaurant. Public relations is about persuasion. It's about sharing important information and making friends with the media people.

PR is generally done by sending newsworthy information to the local TV station, radio station, newspaper, or local food blogger in the form of a Press Release. A newsworthy event can be anything from the opening of your restaurant, to the hiring of a new chef or even a new seasonal menu item. PR is free, but not easy for a rookie to do.

Here's how PR works. You make a list of the food related media people in your area and start sending them newsworthy information that they can write or talk about.

Imagine, that your restaurant has just won a local food or bar competition or something like that. You could write a Press Release and send it to all the local news outlets. If the local TV station is having a slow news day, they might pick up the phone and ask you a few questions. If they are doing a similar story, they may send a film crew over to ask you some questions, and, you just might end up on the 6:00 news.

Here's an interesting point. The people who write articles for newspapers and magazines need something to write about. Another way to say that is they need information to write articles about. If they can get you to send them good information or write the articles for them, that is even better. The truth is that print media is dying, there have been many, many jobs and positions eliminated in recent years. So, the people who still work for these businesses have to pull more than their share of the load. This means that writers are spread thin, very thin. This means that if you have a compelling story, with high resolution photographs, they just might publish your stuff.

I once had a two-page center spread in Delta Sky Magazine (every Delta jet for two months) because I sent them a great article with great pictures. Their original lead story missed the deadline. They were scrambling to fill the hole, and there I was! Florida Senator Connie Mack (a good customer at the time), saw it and sent me a copy with a nice note.

The Press Release is a great free way to spread your message, if you can persuade the media to use it.

Social Media

Facebook, Twitter, Email, Texting, Instagram, Pinterest, Four Square, and so on. Social media is a great way to bypass traditional marketing and take your message directly to your friends, relatives, followers, and customers. The good thing is, that you can talk directly to your customer. The bad news is, that you have to build your own following which takes time, lots of time.

Social media is the hottest and biggest trend in business. You must learn to use social media effectively, or you will be left out in the cold! You should only use the social media tools that make sense for your type of restaurant and customer. Don't wear yourself out trying to use them all.

I would pick one or maybe two and use them consistently. Think of the social media channels as you would print advertising. You can't afford to be in every magazine, newspaper and church bulletin, because you don't have the cash. Although most social media is free, it still requires your TIME, and time is the most precious and valuable resource on Earth!

The Restaurant Website

The closest you will ever come to perfection is on your website! This is your online home. This is where you can tell YOUR complete story in your own words without interruption or space limitation. Be sure to have great pictures and give your potential customers the information they need. This includes your menus, a map to find you, your phone number, your email address, Facebook link, Twitter link, and maybe even a way for your customers to make an online reservation.

Your Facebook Page

After your website, this is your second online information hub. Facebook is a great tool for building loyal followers and communicating with your customers. The rules of Facebook change often, and it is a good idea to have someone who is well versed in social marketing help you set up your page and get started. There is a big difference between using Facebook to keep up with friends and using it to drive customers to your restaurant.

Facebook is a modern marvel. Everybody is on Facebook. Today, customers are using Facebook instead of the phone to communicate with us. Some people try to make reservations through Facebook. This means you better have your hostess plug into Facebook frequently.

The Sales Engine

My goal is to eliminate traditional (expensive) marketing. This requires a strong Ground Game and Social Marketing Program. We must know who our customers are and be able to connect with them via (inexpensive) social marketing. The marketing team must deliver the message and the service team must deliver the Customer Promise.

Expert Marketing / Gravitational Marketing

If you own a restaurant, you are an expert in the world of food and beverage. If you are a really good cook or bartender, you can and should share your knowledge with your customers. This could happen on your Facebook page, web site, weekly blog post, and/or press release.

Be Creative

Personally, I've tried every form of marketing there is. Yes, I even pay a kid $25 an hour to walk around downtown in a chicken suit and hand out coupons to build my lunch business. This is the best form of marketing ever!

Use your brain. Social media is in its infancy. The best ways to use social media haven't been thought of or dreamed up yet. Why can't you be the person who invented the best thing yet?

Remember, marketing is telling people why they will love your restaurant. Your job is to tell your personal and unique story to your market through your website, Facebook page, Twitter, and Instagram. You can even use a kid in a chicken suit, the choice of media is up to you.

Managing Your Online Information

If your restaurant has been around for a while, chances are that you have some misinformation in the cyber world that is confusing your customers. Here's a great idea, make believe you are a potential customer. Google your restaurant. Then, follow the path as a customer would take.

- Is the information that you find about your restaurant accurate and up to date?
- Are your menus up to date, on the various platforms?
- Are the pictures current, or really old and outdated?
- Call your restaurant occasionally to see how your people are answering the phone.
- Listen to the voicemail message, does it need updating?

- Look at the front of your restaurant, how does it look?
- Is your sign well lit, or do you have burned out light bulbs?
- Is your menu board up to date, or old and weathered?

The point of this message is to look at your business as a customer would and clean up the path from their cell phone to your door. Fix, update, and improve everything the customer sees. Improve the stuff you can control. Yes, I know there is some stuff you can't fix, like bad Yelp reviews... c'est la vie!

Marketing & Sales

Most people call it Sales & Marketing, I call it Marketing & Sales, because marketing happens first, and sales happen second.

I break this down into two parts:

1. The Air Campaign (Marketing)
2. The Ground Game (Sales)

Think of Marketing as the Air Campaign that gets the customer to your door. Think of Sales as the Ground Game, the one-on-one selling that happens inside your restaurant, at the table.

To get the second 10% sales increase, you need to do two things:

1. Increase the number of customers by 5%
2. Increase the average check by 5%

If you increase the number of people who eat in your restaurant by 5% AND increase your average check by 5%. Your sales will grow by 10% and you will be headed toward greatness.

The greatest marketing campaign in the world can't help a poorly-run restaurant.

The Air Campaign

The "Air Campaign" is the one-to-many marketing, it includes all forms of advertising and social media. The Air Campaign gets the customer to the door of your restaurant. The Goal of the Air Campaign is to put "butts in the seats" using the following media:

1. Your Website
2. Social Media
3. Traditional Advertising
4. Public Relations
5. Word of Mouth

Your Marketing Must Create Heat!

You must create a product that your CORE audience can't live without! Then you must create HEAT to sell it! Your product must create a buzz, energy, word of mouth, AND customers! If your marketing doesn't create customers, it's useless!

Think of the energy and buzz that Apple creates when they launch a new iPhone. Think of the buzz the NFL creates about the Super Bowl each year. Think of the HEAT that Victoria Secret creates when they roll out a new line of underwear.

Great marketing creates interest, energy, and excitement. Great marketing gets people to talk about your restaurant. Great marketing is about creating a buzz about the core elements of your business. Great marketing gets people to the door of your restaurant.

Here's a fun point... so pay attention! Most marketing is written NOT to piss off the audience. It's true, most marketers are afraid to do anything fun or radical because they are afraid to offend the people who will see or hear it. Because of this, most ads are as boring as vanilla pudding.

Think of how you describe your restaurant or one of your dishes or drinks to a really close friend. You are candid, authentic and genuine, right? That is how you should speak to your customers. Ok, maybe you reduce some of the words that start with the letter F.

The Sales Funnel

There are two major parts of your sales funnel:

1. Marketing gets people to your door
2. The Sales Team makes the sale & keeps the customer coming back.

The goal is to get people into your sales funnel. The top arrows represent NEW people who enter your sales funnel. They come from three places:

1. Positive Word of Mouth
2. Social Media
3. Advertising

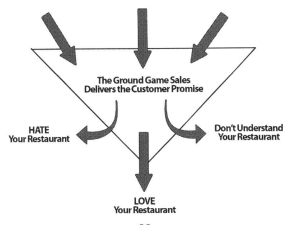

The Marketing Rule of Thirds

I believe in the "Marketing Rule of Thirds". The marketing rule of thirds states, if you know who you are and take a firm stance:

- 1/3 of your new customers will HATE your restaurant.
- 1/3 of your new customers will LOVE your restaurant.
- 1/3 of your new customers will not get it or care either way.

This may seem terrible on the surface, but it is a great thing. Companies like Harley Davidson exemplify the rule of thirds. Donald Trump is a great example of the rule of thirds. People are strongly *for* or strongly *against* them.

Your job is to get the 1/3 who LOVE your restaurant to come back and bring their friends! Your job is to give the 1/3 of the people who LOVE your restaurant more of what they love. You cannot worry about the 2/3's who do not understand or like you. Just find ways to add value to your core customers, the people who LOVE you.

The Ground Game

The "Ground Game" happens INSIDE your restaurant. This is when your people interact with the customer. The ground game is the one on one SELLING that happens at the table.

The goal of the Ground Game is to:

- Deliver the Customer Promise
- Increase the Average Check
- Get Customers in the Club
- Get the Customer to Return and Bring Their Friends
- Reward the Customer for Being Loyal

An effective Ground Game can reduce or eliminate the need for expensive traditional advertising. Instead of giving marketing dollars to TV, radio, and newspaper people (who rarely, if ever, eat at my restaurant), I prefer to use this money to reward my loyal customers with special deals and privileges. The key word here is "reward", not discount.

Remember this, if your marketing gets the customer to the door, and the restaurant team fails to deliver the customer promise, you will lose. If you promise the best cheeseburger in the world, and it doesn't live up to the hype—you're dead!

From this moment forward, your job and the job of your entire team is to improve the quality of the customer experience. It is your duty is to improve the quality of everything the customer sees, touches and tastes in your restaurant. This is called innovation.

The greatest marketing strategy in the world is to create happy customers. Happy customers will spread the good word about your restaurant, and this will radiate positive energy throughout the land, AND your sales will grow by leaps and bounds.

Epitomize Your Core Concept

If you remember our Cheeseburger Restaurant, we aim our core product at our target market (the people who love burgers), we don't worry about the other two thirds (the vegans and vegetarians) who are not our market.

- If you are a burger joint, be a burger joint.
- If you are a taco bar, be a taco bar.

Everything that you do must support your CORE CONCEPT. There should be no mistake about what you are trying to be or do. This is about taking things away and getting focused on the core elements of your concept.

Smart restaurateurs focus on the things that make them different and special, they focus on their Unique Selling Proposition (USP).

Improve, eliminate or change everything that doesn't fit the core concept. Improve the menu, improve the staff, the uniforms, your point of sale marketing, your table tents and interior signage. Improve your store front signage. Make everything line up with your CORE CONCEPT.

Sell Your Brand

Selling your brand starts when the customer walks in the door and sits down at the table, this is the time to really pour it on.

Play Show & Tell

Use your brand name, "Thank you for coming and welcome to Graze! We are excited to have you!" "Let me show and tell you all about Graze!" The goal is to teach each and every customer why you are the best choice for them in the market. I hope you get the idea.

Clean, Safe & Comfortable Place

Set the stage. Improve and upgrade everything the customer sees, tastes, touches, hears, and smells. Clean and paint everything. Rearrange the furniture, fix every piece of broken equipment, and replace every burned-out light bulb. Actually, switch to LED. Let your employees and customers know something new and exciting is happening.

Create Repeat Business

Your servers, bartenders, hosts, and managers are your "Sales Force". Every employee and manager is responsible for creating and building *repeat business!*

Marketing Smarter

As we have previously discussed, new customers generally follow the Rule of Thirds: one third love you, one third hate you, and one third just don't get it.

Most restaurants are satisfied with any type of customer. Most restaurant marketers use the "shotgun approach", they blast the entire market. Smart marketers us a smaller gun with a scope and a laser to hit the *right* targets within the general market. GREAT marketers *attract* the right customers instead of having to *targeting* them.

Here's another important point: You must get the people who LOVE your restaurant to come back again and again. You cannot afford to let them get away... You must turn them into *repeat customers!*

Imagine, what would happen if you could get 33% of all your NEW customers to become regular customers who return 4 to 6 times a year!

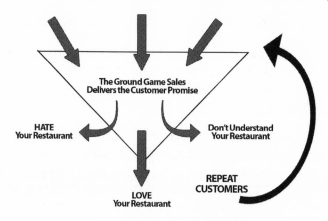

Changing Customer Habits

Most people who dine in any restaurant never return. We know that 2/3's of the people do not return because they hate it, or don't get it. But what about the people who really like or love it? Well, most of them forget about you and go back to their normal routine, and they never return.

I believe customers have THREE restaurants that they visit on a regular basis. They select these places based on, convenience, ambiance, service or whatever, but the point is they are in the HABIT of going to three places.

Your goal as a restaurant owner is to get people to CHANGE THEIR HABIT and put you on their list of three places. The way to do this is to make friends with them and keep in touch with them. Smart restaurant owners invite their customers to come back, and they give them some great REASONS to return.

The Restaurant Club

The restaurant club is the perfect tool to build repeat customers. A restaurant club is a loyalty program that helps you reward your REPEAT customers. A Restaurant club is based on the concept of "Permission Marketing", which means your customers give you permission to communicate with them.

This means the customer LIKES you enough to give you their email address and phone number. Here's How You Start a Club:

- Decide what benefits or rewards you want to offer.
- Print enrollment forms.
- Invite your customers to join.

A club will help you know who your customers are, allow you to keep in touch with them, and reward them for their loyalty. A club allows you to communicate DIRECTLY to your customers.

With their personal information, you will be able to bypass traditional media and even social media. A club is the best way to market directly to your club members through an email and or text program. A club is the best way to build a PERSONAL relationship with your customers.

Never abuse people's private information. Your job is to treat them like a valued friend—not exploit them.

Better People Build Better Clubs

I give great rewards to my club members. I also send them periodic newsletters and special offers. I keep them updated as to what's new and let them know they are APPRECIATED. I give them FREE Stuff on their birthday. I give them FREE stuff for spending money. I throw FREE parties for my BEST club members and BIGGEST spenders. I love my Club Members!

Keeping Your Customers & Club Members

Every time a customer returns to your restaurant you have to deliver the customer promise again. That's right, you must RE-EARN their business, loyalty and support. There are no free passes. You must always treat them with respect and deliver first class hospitality. To keep your customers, you must give them great service and legendary hospitality. You must make them feel special, every time they visit.

Be sure to, ask yourself often, how can we improve and add value to the dining experience? What else can we do to improve the customer experience and keep them coming back?

80% of your future business will come from your current customers. If you deliver the Customer Promise, your satisfied customers will come back for more and... they will bring their friends and family with them.

The Goal is to Create & Keep Your Customers

You will create customers by figuring out what your market wants and giving it to them. You must sell something the market wants to buy and have the guts to CHARGE FULL PRICE!

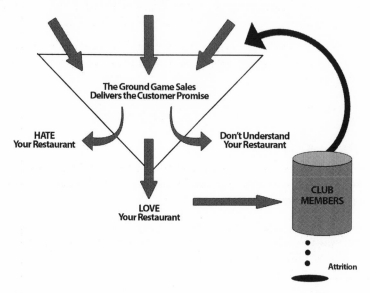

Create Customer Advocates

People who love you and your restaurant will bring their friends. They will tell everyone they know about your restaurant. They may even invest in your next restaurant venture.

Have you ever asked your customers to refer you to their friends, or bring their friends with them? Why not? Your customers have tons of friends, and they would love to turn them on to their favorite restaurant. All you have to do is ask.

Reward your customer advocates for bringing their friends and associates! Give extra points to club members or a promotional gift certificate for bringing in NEW CUSTOMERS.

When someone brings their friends, you better make a BIG DEAL out of it. You better make them, and their friends, feel SPECIAL! This is the time for your hospitality to kick in and make the person who referred you look and feel like a "rock star". Nothing could be worse than bragging up your favorite restaurant and telling people how much "this restaurant loves me". Then, upon arrival, you get treated like shit by the staff, what a shame!

The goal is to make your customer advocates look and feel like the very important people that they are! If you and your people can do this consistently, you will all get rich!

The Goal is to create "Wow!" Experiences for everyone you serve, AND get people into your club, AND keep them coming back, AND encourage them to bring their friends. I find that rewarding repeat customers inspires them to spend more money on each visit, it also helps to turn them into Customer Advocates, which has great long-term value. The most effective form of marketing is positive word of mouth from Customer Advocates! 80% of your future business will come from REPEAT CUSTOMERS.

I would be happy to help you set up an effective club, just email me and we can get started. Each of my restaurants have over 15,000 club members. I am the club Master!

Increase The Average Check

This is a really important section, so pay attention...

Increasing the average check starts with staff training and coaching. This does not happen all by itself. You must teach your managers and waiters to go beyond just taking the order.

We call them waiters, servers and sales people, not order takers. Good waiters use the up-sell, the bump and the add-on, to increase the check average, which usually increases their tips. As of this writing, TIPS are still a thing in the good ol' USA.

Good waiters must sell entrees, appetizers, side dishes, the second round of drinks, the second bottle of wine, desserts, coffee and cordials.

I know you have heard this before, but the question is, are your waiters up-selling or is everybody just going through the motions? Do you have a training system in place to reward the waiters, servers and sales people who really sell?

Let me ask you this:

- Do you know what your average check is?
- Do you know who your top two and bottom two salespeople are?
- Are you teaching your people how to sell more to each customer and each table?
- If Yes, how can you improve it and do it even better?

If you are *not* working with your wait staff and bartenders to up-sell, you are killing yourself. This is like committing suicide. It's ridiculous and self-destructive. I know what you are saying, I can hear you all the way over here in Iowa City. You are saying that you have delegated this responsibility to your managers. You are trying *not* to be a micromanager.

Please allow me to tell you something important... The restaurant business is a micro-business. And if you are *not* a micromanager, you will *not* be in the restaurant business for very long.

Here's the problem: When it comes to selling, most restaurant managers confuse their people. They talk about selling appetizers, special features, desserts, wine, cocktails and after drinks. They tell them to get people to join the club and sign up for the next wine dinner. They have contests to see who can sell the most desserts, the most appetizers and certain types of wine or cocktails.

They teach them WHAT to sell. They don't teach them HOW to sell. This leads to serious frustration on the part of both the manager and the waiter. This happens because most restaurant managers don't know how to break the sales process into an actionable sequence that any person with a 5th grade education can understand.

The second problem is that the goal is to increase their AVERAGE check. Yes, this is one of the Six Ways to Increase Sales, however; the way we get there is not a straight line and most waiters can't figure this out on their own. The main reason that most managers and waiters can't figure it out on their own is because they don't spend enough time studying it. Their thinking is usually, this is just a J.O.B, and you're lucky I showed up today.

The posted goal is to INCREASE THE AVERAGE CHECK. A good waiter will take everybody's drink order, then recommend ways to bump them or upgrade them. They will recommend Jack Daniels or Tito's but that's about the end of it. Then, after they serve the drinks, a good waiter will take the food order and recommend ways to add on. This is pretty typical.

Most waiters struggle trying to make all these recommendations. They recommend wine to people who want to drink beer or cocktails. They try to sell a spicy appetizer to older people and get turned down. Then, when it comes time for dessert, the waiter has made up their mind that these people are just unsophisticated and cheap, so they give it a half assed attempt to no avail.

Five-Step Sales Process

Here's what I teach my people, and it really works. There are five steps to the sales process, if you miss any of these steps you will not make the sale. Here they are:

1. Qualify the Table
2. Be a Professional Sales Person
3. Build Rapport
4. Inform & Educate
5. Ask For & Close the Sale

Qualify the Table

Who are these people and why are they here? Are they a group of 20-somethings celebrating an important social event? A young family with a baby stroller? A group of business people, or a couple on a first date? Each of these groups will require a different attitude and style of service.

Be a Professional Sales Person

You must look & act the part, and display great service, skill, and technique. You must also be able to adjust your role based on the people at your table. If you have four tables, you may have to play four different roles. You must become a chameleon.

Build Rapport

This is when you connect with your customer. This is when you make them feel special and important. This is about delivering the level of professionalism and hospitality that is warranted with this group of people. You might even have to play a slightly different role for the various people at each table. For example, a gruff business person will require a different type of attention and service than their underlings, or a couple on a hot date.

Inform & Educate

This is when you show them you know your stuff. This is when you display knowledge of the food and drink menu. This is when you explain what everything is and why it is the perfect choice for them. Here's the catch, if the customer asks you a question and you don't know the answer, or just make up some BS, you are dead meat! When it comes time to SELL something, they will not be interested because you have lost your credibility. Know your stuff!

When the customer sees you as the expert and asks for your opinion, this is when you can really up-sell and show them a great time.

Ask For & Close the Sale

If you have checked all four of the boxes above in the mind of the customer, you become a trusted advisor and culinary guide. This is the best situation for you to sell, because they trust you.

Become a Trusted Advisor

You must teach your servers to care about their customers and guide them to the best dining experience possible. Your people must show the customers the best way to experience and enjoy your restaurant to the fullest. Waiters must become experts at guiding your guests toward a great experience. This is a blend of hospitality & tour guide.

It's not about upselling; it's about creating a great dining experience for the guest. The goal is to *add value* to the dining experience! The best way to add value and upsell is to think of your customers as the important and valuable clients that they are.

Imagine, if your mother or some very important person came to your restaurant, what would you want them to experience? You would want them to experience the BEST you have to offer, right? You would want them to experience the BEST thing for the occasion. That is how you should approach every single table that comes to your restaurant!

One of my restaurants is Martini's Grille in Burlington Iowa. It is The Place to Celebrate Life in that part of the world. People save their money, so they can celebrate a special event at this amazing restaurant.

Martini's has Three Very Important Responsibilities:

1. We have a moral obligation to insure that guest has the BEST possible dining experience.
2. We owe every customer excellent food, drinks and service.
3. We must do everything possible to help the restaurant thrive and stay in business.

If we miss the mark, the people who live in that area will not have a first-class restaurant to go to. I'm not being pompous, arrogant, or funny. This restaurant has been in Burlington, Iowa for 22 years and it is very important to the people in our little community. I personally see it as my sworn duty to take care of them. This may sound crazy to you, but it is really real to me.

Ok, so now that we have unpacked all that, the point is that we have a moral obligation to our valuable clients. It's is our duty to insure they have a great time. Let's move forward.

Turn Every Four-Top into a Five-Top

The average restaurant gets a lot of four-top tables over the course of a year. Imagine what would happen if you could turn every four-top into a five-top without having to make room for the extra person.

To increase the average sale, we change the game. We forget about the average check and work on maximizing the dining experience for the individual and the group. We read the people at the table and figure out who they are and why they are here. Then, we design a dining experience that is tailor made just for them.

Your people need simple and actionable tactics & techniques to follow. Here are a few simple techniques that you can teach your people to use at every table to add value to the dining experience and increase your average check.

A great waiter works to sell to both the individual customer and the table. They take the order and then step back to look at the big picture. They make specific recommendations that make sense for the table. This usually involves getting the individual customers to SHARE something as a table.

The graphic below shows a table with four customers. In the example each customer has purchased one entrée for $20 and one drink for $6, the total sale per person is $26. The grand total for the table is $104.

The Average Check

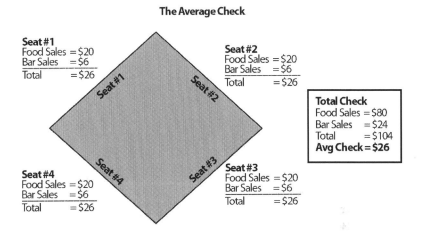

Seat #1
Food Sales = $20
Bar Sales = $6
Total = $26

Seat #2
Food Sales = $20
Bar Sales = $6
Total = $26

Total Check
Food Sales = $80
Bar Sales = $24
Total = $104
Avg Check = $26

Seat #4
Food Sales = $20
Bar Sales = $6
Total = $26

Seat #3
Food Sales = $20
Bar Sales = $6
Total = $26

Opportunity #1: Sell the Second Drink

The biggest opportunity in a restaurant is to sell them a second drink or a nice glass of wine. Most people like to have two drinks with dinner, or a cocktail and a glass of wine. I don't know about you, but my friends like to drink, catch a buzz and have a good time, AND they hate to go home stone sober. Hey, it's the truth. This is why the world invented Uber.

If your customers like to drink and have fun, be sure that they get enough to drink. I'm not talking about being irresponsible and getting them hammered. I'm talking about making sure they have a good time.

Come on, we have all gone out to dinner and can't get a drink when we need one. It sucks, and it's one of the main reasons some customers don't come back.

It's a damn shame. Here we are trying to increase sales, and there they are trying to spend their money and have fun, and we can't get them a drink. This hurts us TWICE! We miss a sale, they don't get their drink, and they don't come back. Ouch.

If you could sell each person a second drink in this example, the sales total for the table would increase from $104 to $128 and the average check would go from $26 to $32 per person. That's a 23% increase. If only 20% of your tables get a second drink, **your sales will increase by 5%**.

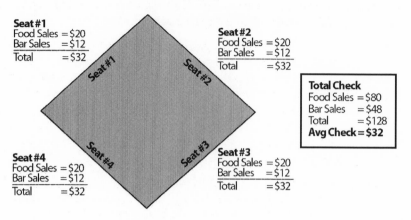

Seat #1		
Food Sales	=	$20
Bar Sales	=	$12
Total	=	$32

Seat #2		
Food Sales	=	$20
Bar Sales	=	$12
Total	=	$32

Total Check		
Food Sales	=	$80
Bar Sales	=	$48
Total	=	$128
Avg Check	=	**$32**

Seat #4		
Food Sales	=	$20
Bar Sales	=	$12
Total	=	$32

Seat #3		
Food Sales	=	$20
Bar Sales	=	$12
Total	=	$32

Opportunity #2: Appetizers

The easiest way to sell appetizers is to get the table to share one or two. Sharing is fun! When you go out for dinner, don't you like share some appetizers with your friends? I sure do! It makes the experience more fun! If you want your customers to have a better dining experience, make sure they start by sharing some delicious appetizers.

The best way to sell appetizers is to be smart and patient. Here's one way to look at the order process. Most people stress out over their entrée decision for one of three reasons:

1. We want to make the perfect choice
2. We want to stay within our budget
3. We want to stay within our diet

As soon as we make the entrée choice, we sit back and relax, AND we lower our guard. A smart waiter will wait until after the table has made their entrée choices, and then they will recommend a specific appetizer for the table to share. A smart waiter might say, "Would you like to SHARE our homemade pretzels with warm cheese fondue while you are waiting for your salads?"

This could be any appetizer or sharable dish, such as a pizza, a sushi roll, guacamole, hummus, or anything specific that is designed to be shared. Of course, it works best if it's a "House Specialty".

As we just discussed, most people find the "What am I going to order?" decision a bit stressful. Everybody wants to order something they will love, and most people have one of two problems when they order in a restaurant (the first is price, and the second is calories).

After they make the Big Decision, they relax and lower their guard. This is the PERFECT time to sell something extra to the table. When you get them to share, the table picks up the extra cost and the extra calories, and you also get the SHARING thing to happen. People love to share! Sharing adds FUN, which adds VALUE to their dining experience!

The Outback used to use this appetizer selling technique to perfection with their Bloomin' Onion. First, they used their Air Campaign to bombard us with Bloomin' Onion ads on a regular basis. Then right after we ordered our steak, the server always asked, "Would you care to share our famous Bloomin' Onion as an appetizer while you are waiting for your salads?" It's the perfect "1-2 Punch". Boom! After each member of the table has ordered their entrée & sides is the *perfect opportunity* to increase your sales and add value Do not miss it.

I believe your staff can accomplish this sale at 33% of your tables, if you coach them. All you need is a GREAT "shareable" appetizer to sell, and an eager kitchen staff, ready to crank them out. If you can sell the second drink AND get the table to share a $12 appetizer, your numbers would look like the chart below:

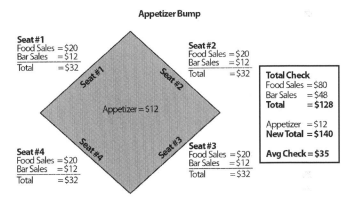

Appetizer Bump

Seat #1
Food Sales = $20
Bar Sales = $12
Total = $32

Seat #2
Food Sales = $20
Bar Sales = $12
Total = $32

Appetizer = $12

Seat #4
Food Sales = $20
Bar Sales = $12
Total = $32

Seat #3
Food Sales = $20
Bar Sales = $12
Total = $32

Total Check
Food Sales = $80
Bar Sales = $48
Total = $128

Appetizer = $12
New Total = $140

Avg Check = $35

To Recap

The check average example started at $26. When we added the second drink and the shareable appetizer the average is check went up to $35. The total bill for the table went from $104 to $140. That's a $36 increase and a 33% improvement. Wow!

These simple moves also work great for dessert. The best part of selling dessert is that it opens up the magic vault to after-dinner coffee and cordials. This is how you can turn a four-top into a five-top. If you can sell the second drink and an appetizer or a dessert to just 20% of your tables, you will get a 5% ground game sales increase. When you combine the 5% ground game sales increase with 5% more customers, you will have your SECOND 10% sales increase.

It really is this easy. All you have to do is create the plan, train your staff, then FOCUS, FOCUS, FOCUS!

Chapter Recap

The key concepts in this chapter are:

- The Goal is TWO 10% Sales Increases In the Next 90 Days
- Six Ways to Increase Sales
- Use the Rule of Thirds To Speak to Your Core Audience
- Epitomize Your Concept
- Start a Restaurant Club
- Understand and Maximize The Market, The Message & The Media
- Improve Your Air Campaign – One-to-Many Marketing
- Master the Ground Game – One on One Selling that Happens at the Table
- Become a Trusted Advisor
- Turn Every Four-Top into a Five-Top

While the ideas in this chapter are still fresh in your mind. I want you to STOP READING and make a list of 10 ways that you can Increase Sales. This is a Leadership Activity that is IMPORTANT, but not URGENT. Don't put this off. Do it NOW.

I have divided this section into two parts. Five Ways to get MORE customers to the restaurant, and Five Ways to INCREASE the average check size.

Five Ways You Can Get New Customers to the Restaurant:

Five Ways You Can Increase the Average Check:

Fundamental # 6:
Build a Money Management System

Sustainable local food is really a cool thing that lots of chefs and restaurant owners are really excited about these days. But, do you know what's even cooler? Long-term, sustainable profit!

The fact is that business exists to create a profit for the owner and investors. If you can't make money, you will die. The way to make money is by adding value to your business, your people, and your customers.

Think about all the money that has gone through your restaurant over the years. Imagine what could have happened if you could have saved just 1% of that money. Think of all the money that you have pissed away AND allowed your managers and employees to piss away or steal. The thought is depressing. It makes me really angry when I think about what COULD have been done better and smarter.

Well ladies and gentlemen, there is no use crying over spilled milk. The past is in the past and we can't do anything about it. The present and the future however; are something we can do something about. The goal of this chapter is to help you build wealth. Starting right now, I want you to understand rule #1 of Money Management:

Rule #1: Sales must be GREATER than expenses.

If you want a 10% profit, sales must be 10% greater than expenses. There are two types of expenses in your restaurant.

1. Things that are *mission critical*, that move you toward the goal.
2. Things that are *nice to have*, that make life easy and comfortable.

The things we need are like muscle and bone. The other things are fat. If you want to win, you must cut the fat and only invest in muscle and bone. Easy to say, hard to do. It's really is an easy decision, above the line is muscle and bone. Below the line is fat. Which will you choose? Which will your managers choose? Let's get started on this exciting fundamental.

It's Time To Talk About Money...
Your Money.

A restaurant is a business, and the goal of business is to build wealth for the shareholders. The problem is, most independent restaurant owners have an "artist mentality". They get into the business because they are in love with their product or service.

As we have discussed, the key to success in our business is to BALANCE all of the Eight Basic Fundamentals.

The goal of this "money chapter" is to help you earn a 10% profit, which is the Gold Standard in the restaurant business. The objective is for you to have all your taxes paid on time, and a ZERO accounts payable balance.

My real goal is for you to take home 10% of your net sales, every year for the next ten years. This fundamental is a simple black-and-white science. In order to make a ten percent profit, your sales must be 10% GREATER than your expenses. If you are already doing this, you are a star! If you are not, keep reading.

10% may not seem like much of a profit to you, but did you know that the profit of the average McDonalds is only about 5%? When you look at a 10% Profit as a rate of return on your investment, it can be awesome.

Manage the Money

Only 14% of all restaurants are making money, and only the top 5% earn a 10% profit. In fact, 80% of all restaurant owners in America can't pay their bills on time, and they survive by "robbing Peter to pay Paul". The mortality rate of restaurants is very high.

86% of restaurants don't live to see their fifth birthday. This means, 86% of all the people who invest their life savings in a restaurant, walk away broke and embarrassed in less than five years.

This breaks my heart! Here are some interesting statistics:

- 26% of restaurants fail in the first year.
- 19% fail in the second year.
- 60% don't live to see their third birthday.
- 86% don't live to see their fifth birthday.
- Only 14% make it to five years.
- 5% of restaurants make it to ten years.
- 1% of restaurants thrive!

Here's some more statistics:

- 40% of restaurants lose money.
- 40% break even.
- 14% profit between 1% - 9%.
- 5% make over a 10% profit.
- 1% of restaurants earn 11% or more.

My goal is help you see the overall concept of how money works in your restaurant, and help you build a smart financial plan, so you can live the life of your dreams and retire with a BIG smile on your face. The goal of this chapter is to help you BUILD WEALTH!

What's Holding You Back

Your Thinking & Actions are what's holding you back from making a 10% Profit. Before we dig in to this important chapter, I want you to know that money management is about executing time-tested basic fundamentals. These are not new wave, high-finance, techniques that require an MBA to manage. If you can do 5th grade math, you can manage the finances of a restaurant.

It is one thing to understand these fundamentals, it is another thing to actually USE them. And, it is an even better thing to use these fundamentals, AND teach them to your managers and employees, so they can help you Build Wealth!

The ideas that follow will work for you, if you are smart enough to USE them. The key is to take action. If your restaurant is losing money, or just breaking even, something needs to CHANGE, and that change must begin with YOU... right now.

As You Think, So Shall You Be

What crazy ideas do you believe?

- We used to believe the world was flat.
- We used to believe the Earth was the center of the Universe.
- We used to believe man could not run a "four-minute mile".

On May 5, 1954, the world record for running a mile was four minutes and one second. Running a mile in under 4 minutes, was considered IMPOSSIBLE, because people were not designed to run that fast.

On May 6, 1954, Roger Bannister ran the mile in **3 minutes, 59.4 seconds**. The world learned that running the mile in under 4-minute mile WAS possible. Over the next year, Bannister's record was beaten, several times.

As of this writing, the record is **3 minutes 43.13 seconds**, almost 17 seconds faster than the impossible.

What's Possible?

I'm here to tell you that earning a 10% profit in your restaurant is possible, if you make it a priority and build an effective money management system.

Think about it: You are the boss. You are the leader. It's up to you to set the goal and make it happen.

In cooking, we use a specific recipe for each dish. In business, the recipe is called a system. When your cooking knowledge & skills improve, your dishes will become more consistent and delicious. The same thing happens with a money management system: When your systems improve, your profit will improve. 80% of all restaurant systems are designed to break even or lose money. Only 5% of restaurant systems are purposefully designed to earn a 10% profit.

The Profit & Loss Statement

The P&L statement is the financial document that restaurant people are the most familiar with. In this section, I will show you what your costs are supposed to be.

Cost Management is simple, you figure out what you want your costs to be and then create a system to make it Happen!

In the restaurant business, we have three major cost categories:

1. Cost of Goods
2. Cost of Labor
3. Other Cost

Most people forget about the PROFIT category until it's too late. I believe, profit must be built into the system at the beginning.

Our goal is to earn a 10% profit, so we need to keep that in mind. However; you must not turn into single minded, greedy monster, who only cares about money. You must remember that profit is PART of a well-balanced operating system, and a professionally run restaurant.

To be successful, you must execute ALL EIGHT of the Basic Fundamentals AND Deliver the Customer Promise.

Understanding 30-30-30-10

The goal of the P&L is to achieve 30-30-30-10 Standard. This refers to the percentage of sales that you can spend in each category. If you are a little high in one category you must be a little lower in another category to achieve the gold standard: 10% Profit.

On the next page is an example of a P&L, it shows the various line items that fall under each of the main cost categories. The example restaurant has $1,000,000 in sales and has achieved the gold standard, 10% profit.

Restaurant Sales

Bar Sales	$300,000	
Food Sales	$700,000	
Total Sales	$1,000,000	100%

Cost of Goods

Bar Cost	$75,000	
Food Cost	$225,000	
Total Cost of Goods	$300,000	30%

Labor Costs

Bar / Dining Room	$100,000	
Kitchen	$120,000	
Management	$50,000	
Payroll Taxes	$30,000	
Total Labor Costs	$300,000	30%

Other Costs (Fixed & Variable)

Rent / Mortgage	$60,000	
Utilities	$20,000	
Insurance	$12,000	
Credit Card Fees -2%	$20,000	
Legal / CPA	$6,000	
Trash Removal	$2,000	
Restaurant Supplies	$30,000	
Cleaning Supplies	$14,000	
Linen & Laundry	$15,000	
Office Supplies	$6,000	
Repairs & Maintenance	$10,000	
Sales & Marketing	$35,000	
Comp Expense	$70,000	
Total Other Costs	$300,000	30%

Profit	$100,000	10%

Your Current Numbers

Let's take a look at your numbers. Below is a self-examination that you can use to see how your business compares to the 30-30-30-10. Take a look at your year to date profit & loss statement and write in your current year to date numbers in the box below.

Be sure you have at least 3 months of data, otherwise use your P&L from last year. You do have a P&L, don't you?

Your Numbers

SALES	$_____	
Cost of Goods	$_____	____%
Labor Cost	$_____	____%
Other Cost	$_____	____%
TOTAL EXPENSES	$_____	____%
PROFIT	$_____	____%

Compare your current numbers to the 30-30-30-10 above. If you are at a ten percent profit, you rule! If your numbers are NOT there yet, don't freak out, this is just your starting point. In a few months from now you will be able to look back and see your progress.

Time to Face Reality & Accept Responsibility

This part is very important, pay attention... In fact, please read it twice.

Most restaurant owners and managers never bother to calculate and manage the costs in their restaurant. This happens for several reasons:

Reason #1: They are lazy. They never took the time to learn the basic fundamentals for themselves. They assume that their so-called managers are capable of managing costs and making a profit. This is usually, total B.S.

Reason #2: They know how to cost a menu and manage costs but, have never taken the time to do the hard work associated with understanding and managing costs in their own restaurant. They think, "I'm the owner. I am above that. I have managers to take care of that stuff." Wrong!

Now, you might be asking, "How do I know how much money we can spend on each line item?" Keep this in mind...

The goal is to run a 30-30-30-10. That means that if you have $1,000,000 in sales you can spend 30% or $300,000 in each of the main cost categories and still have a profit of $100,000. Every dollar that you allow your managers to spend above the (30-30-30-100 budget will come from the profit line. Which means it will come out of YOUR POCKET!

You must create a budget and give specific numbers to each department head: The GM, Chef, The Service Manager, and the Bar Manager. The Budget reflects the "Financial Goals" of the business. The budget is the THEORETICAL reflection (in a perfect world) of what can happen if your managers do what they are supposed to do. If you can't make the numbers happen on paper, you will never make them happen in the REAL WORLD!

Theoretical Costs vs Actual Costs

Good operators know what the numbers on the P&L are supposed to be. They have weekly or monthly meetings with managers to discuss the numbers and find ways to hit their goals. In this section, I will show you how to figure what your costs are supposed to be. But it's up to you & your team to make it happen!

- What is Food Cost Supposed to be?
- *What is it in reality?*
- What is Kitchen Labor supposed to be?
- *What is it in reality?*
- How much were we supposed to spend on linen?
- *What did we actually spend?*

Now Hear This: You will NOT achieve the 30-30-30-10 in the first year of a new independent restaurant, no matter how good you think you are.

It will take a few years to get your sales and costs where they need to be. One of the biggest mistakes that owners and investors make is to expect a restaurant to hit their Theoretical numbers and earn a 10% Profit in the first year. This NEVER happens. Success takes time, you must be persistent, you must continually adapt and make adjustments until you figure it out.

"It's unusual & indeed abnormal for a concern to make money during the first several years of existence. The initial product & organization are never right."

    - Harvey Firestone

Breaking Down The 30-30-30-10

Let's dig a little deeper and talk about all the pieces that get us to a 10% Profit, starting with sales.

Sales

Under the sales category we record bar and food sales. These numbers should be tracked separately so we can determine a separate <u>food</u> and <u>beverage</u> cost. Some restaurants also have retail sales (T-shirts, gifts and trinkets), we will not be considering those type of sales in this example.

Cost of Goods

This is a VARIABLE expense, which means it will vary depending on many factors including the amount of sales. If you don't make a sale, you shouldn't buy or use the product. The cost of FOOD should be tracked separately from the cost of BEVERAGE, so you can determine what your cost is for each line item. The chef / kitchen manager is responsible for food cost and the service manager or bar manager is responsible for the bar cost.

Labor Costs

These costs include the Bar, Dining Room, Kitchen, and Management personnel, don't forget Payroll Taxes! The Chef is responsible for Kitchen Labor, and the Service Manager is responsible for Bar/Dining Room Labor and the GM is responsible for everything.

Other Costs

"Other Costs" include everything else. Other Cost is divided into two sections: Fixed "Other Costs" & Variable "Other Costs".

Fixed Other Costs are things we must have no matter what, such as rent or mortgage, utilities, insurance, credit card fees and trash removal.

Variable Other Costs are flexible things that vary from month to month like china, glass, silverware, linen and disposables.

Build the Budget in Reverse Order

In Food Guru World, we build the P&L Backwards. We start with the 10% Profit, then we add Other Costs and Labor Costs. This will tell us how much we have left for Cost of Goods.

- Sales $1,000,000
- *10% Profit*   *$100,000*
- Other Costs $310,000
- Labor Costs $320,000
- ***Remainder*** ***$270,000***

The example above shows what it looks like when we build our financial plan backwards. We start with the SALES and subtract the PROFIT and FIXED EXPENSES (Other Cost and Labor Cost). The remainder is what we have left over for Cost of Goods (Food & Bar Cost).

The restaurant in the above example has $270,000 left over for Cost of Goods. They need to run a 27% for Cost of Goods – if they want to keep a 10% Profit.

The Cost of Goods is the most flexible of the three cost categories. If your restaurant is a landmark with a high mortgage and a high degree of skilled labor and service, you may need to run a lower cost of goods.

This is why dinner is more expensive in a high-end landmark restaurant, than it is at a strip mall. The customer must pay more for the ambiance, elevated service, and overhead. I explore this in more detail in a minute.

The point is that each restaurant is different, and a perfect 30-30-30-10 may not work for your restaurant. Here's another point. It may take you a few years to get your sales to a point where you can achieve the 10% Profit. The important thing is that you build it into the plan and don't settle, until you get there.

Cost of Goods

Your Cost of Goods is determined by what is LEFT OVER after you pay Labor & Other Costs (fixed costs).

Prices in a fine dining restaurant will be higher than in a quick-serve joint. If you have a great location and high rent, your Other Cost will be high. If you offer great service and complex food, your Labor Cost will be high, especially in the early years.

You must make up the difference, and still earn a 10% profit, by running a lower Cost of Goods. When you know what your fixed costs are, you can set portions and prices wherever you choose. Simply put, your vendor determines the product cost, but you determine the quality, preparation, portion and SALES PRICE.

Remember: Prices must be fair to both, the Customer & the Owner.

Pay strict attention to this statement!

You control purchasing. You control receiving and storage. You control the portion and the cost of each menu item. You set the price and the cost percentage for each menu item. You control whether your people follow the recipe/portion control standards or not. Why would you ever let food cost or bar cost be out of line or get out of control?

Think of your food & beverage products as CASH, because they are:

- That's not a T-Bone steak, it's $20
- That's not a pound of shrimp, it's $10
- That's not a bottle of wine, it's $25

When you know what your costs and percentages need to be, it is your responsibility to make it happen. You must "cost out" every food and beverage item that you sell. Costing the menu is a time consuming & an educational experience.

First, you figure out what it costs to make each menu item. Then you set your prices to produce the cost of goods percentage that the budget calls for. This sounds simple because it is! The tricky part is getting the Staff, Employees, and Managers to follow the portion control and recipe standards.

We both know, your people don't care how much money you make, they only care about how much money *they* make, so if you want a 10% profit you must build the profit into the equation. You must think of profit as a FIXED COST. Think of the 10% Profit as *your* salary!

Think about this: If your people don't care about how much money you make, maybe you should think about finding people who *do.*

Restaurant owners have no problem figuring out in advance how much they will pay the cooks and waiters, so don't forget to pay YOURSELF! The Goal of Ownership is to BUILD WEALTH, not destroy it!

Goals for Cost of Goods

Every point or dollar that you are off in the cost categories, comes from Profit! Every dollar that you are off in the cost categories comes from Your Pocket! If you are high in one category you must be lower in another!

As time goes on and sales increase, your fixed costs (OTHER & LABOR) will stabilize and free up cash to help stabilize your COST OF GOODS and increase PROFIT.

Imagine, a restaurant with $1 million in sales, and an average check of $30. Imagine a 70/30 split, which means that 70% of your sales will come from food and 30% will come from beverage sales. The bar cost must be 25% and food cost 32.1% to produce a 30% COMBINED cost of goods (see the numbers below).

Sales	Cost	%
Bar Sales	$300,000	30.0%
Food Sales	$700,000	70.0%
Total Sales	**$1,000,000**	**100%**
Cost of Goods	Cost	%
Bar Cost	$75,000	25.0%
Food Cost	$225,000	32.1%
Total Cost of Goods	**$300,000**	**30%**

Theoretical vs. Actual Cost of Goods

This part here is important AND really hard to do, so pay attention.

Your Theoretical Cost of Goods is what your costs *should* be in a perfect world with no errors or mistakes. But we don't live in a perfect world, so this is the goal we strive to hit in our restaurants.

Your goal is to get Actual Costs as close to your Theoretical costs as possible. This will require serious effort.

To figure your Theoretical Cost of Goods you need to know a few things:

- The Cost to Produce
- The Sales Price
- The Cost Percentage
- The Profit-Margin

...of every menu item that you sell.

Step One – Cost Your Menus

To determine this information, you must cost out every item on your food menu, (appetizers, salads, soups, entrees, dessert, etc.) You must also do this for every bar item that you sell, (beer, wine, mixed drinks and specialty drinks, etc.)

Step Two – Run a Product Mix

You will need a PRODUCT MIX REPORT to tell you how many of each item you have sold. Your POS system should give you these answers. When you know these numbers, you can calculate what your Theoretical Food and Beverage Cost should be.

Step Three – Get the Theoretical To MATCH the Actual

The Goal is to get the Theoretical Cost and the Actual Cost to match. The first time you do this exercise, the difference will be scary... really scary!

Just like any exercise, you will improve with practice and time. This process will force you to focus deeply, which will help you understand your business, and show you where you are leaking serious amounts of CASH!

The Food Cost Process

Let's walk through the process with Food Cost. The Steps in Food Menu Costing are:

1. Document the cost of each food item you purchase
2. Document the Recipe
3. Determine the Portion
4. Determine the Sale Price for each menu item
5. Calculate the Food Cost & percentage for each menu item

The Steps in Getting Theoretical & Actual to Match are:

1. Run the Product Mix Report
2. Calculate Your Theoretical Cost of Goods
3. Compare Your Theoretical to Your Actual Cost of Goods

Document the Cost of Each Item

This is an important project that must be done no matter what. The best place to start is by listing each food item by category (i.e. - meat, produce, dry goods) and breaking them down into usable units or sizes.

For example, we buy random chicken breasts in 40-pound cases, the cost is $80.00 per case. There are 40# of chicken in the case, so $80 divided by 40# = $2.00 per pound.

When we trim the wing fat and scapula tendon from the chicken, we have 10% waste. The $2.00-pound cost x .10% waste = $2.20 per usable pound. This is good information for your cooks, they can see the value of the products they use. Here are some examples:

Food Item	Cost	Pack/Unit Size	Unit Cost	Usable Cost
Chicken Breast	$80.00	40# Case	$2.00 lb	$2.20 lb
13-15 Shrimp	$140.00	5/2# bags	$14.00 lb	$1.00 ea
Hanger Steaks 12oz	$100.00	12/12oz	$8.33 ea	.52 oz
Roma Tomatoes	$30.00	60 count	.50 ea	.20 oz
Peeled Garlic	$12.00	Gallon	.10 oz	.02 tsp
Onions	$25.00	50 # Bag	.30 cup	.04 oz
Red Bell Peppers	$30.00	30 ct case	$1.00 ea	.20 oz
Fresh Basil	$10.00	Pound	.20 oz	.10 Tbsp
Butter	$50.00	36 # case	$1.38 lb	.09 oz
Olive Oil	$25.00	Gallon	.25 oz	.13 Tbsp
Kosher Salt	$2.00	5#	.02 oz	.01 Tbsp
Black Pepper	$25.00	5#	.30 oz	.05 tsp
H&R Flour	$25.00	50#	.50 lb	.03 oz
White Wine	$5.00	25 oz btl	$1.60 cup	.20 oz
Parmesan Cheese	$8.00	pound	$4.00 cup	.50 oz

Document the Recipes

You will need a written recipe for each item on your menu. For example:

Bronzed Chicken Breast:	Portion
Chicken Breast	8 oz
H&R Flour	dredge
Olive Oil	1 oz
Chopped Garlic	1 tsp
Minced Onion	1 Tbsp
White Wine	3 oz
Kosher Salt	1 tsp
Black Pepper	1 tsp
Heavy Cream	1 oz
Butter	2 oz
Diced Roma Tomatoes	1/2 ea
Fresh Basil	1 oz
Shredded Parmesan Cheese	.5 oz

Procedure:

Pound the chicken breast and dredge in flour, reserve. Heat a 10" Skillet to medium high. Add olive oil, swirl to coat the pan. Add chicken breast, cook for 1 minute, flip. Add garlic and onions, cook one minute, deglaze with white wine, season with salt and pepper.

Reduce heat and allow to simmer until chicken breast is cooked through. Remove chicken from pan and place on serving plate. Add cream to the pan and allow to reduce by half. Add butter and stir to incorporate, add tomatoes and fresh basil, stir to incorporate. Pour sauce over chicken breast, top with parmesan, serve immediately.

Cost the Recipes

Here's an example of how to cost a recipe:

Sautéed Chicken Breast	Portion	Cost	Unit	Portion Cost
Chicken Breast	8 oz	2.20 lb	1/2lb	$1.10
Flour	1 oz	.50 lb	.03oz	$0.03
Olive Oil	1 oz	$25 gal	.25oz	$0.25
Chopped Garlic	1 tsp			$0.10
Minced Onion	1 Tbsp			$0.10
White Wine	4 oz	$5 ltr	4oz	$0.60
Kosher Salt	1 tsp			$0.02
Black Pepper	1 tsp			$0.25
Cream	1 oz			$0.20
Butter	2 oz	$1.38 lb	.09oz	$0.18
Roma Tomatoes	.5 ea	$30/60ct	.50ea	$0.25
Fresh Basil	1 oz	$10 lb		$0.20
Cost of the Recipe				$3.28
Waste Factor 5%				$0.16
Total Cost of Recipe				**$3.44**
Sale Price				$15.00
Food Cost %				22.90%
Profit Margin				**$11.66**

In the previous example we determined that it will cost $3.28 to produce this chicken dish, then we added 5% for a waste factor, because there is always waste. This makes the total cost of the dish $3.44. If we price it at $15, the numbers look like this.

- Cost of the Dish $3.44
- Sale Price $15.00
- Food Cost %   22.9%
- **Profit**   **$11.56**

The Wrap Around Cost

Some restaurants offer things like bread & butter, soup and salad, and a side dish FREE with the entrée. These extra items are called a "Wrap Around".

To determine the wrap around, you must determine what it costs to produce these FREE ITEMS and then add the WRAP AROUND COST, to the cost of each entrée. This may be done by one of two ways:

1. Determine how much you spend every week on bread, butter salad and side dishes. Then divide that number by the number of entrees you serve, to get the average wrap around costs per customer. *(Example: $2,000 spent on wrap around items / 1,000 customers = $2.00 per customer.)*
2. Determine how much each side item costs. Determine how much a portion of the free items cost. Have the servers ring the free side items in with the entrée as a zero charge (The kitchen needs this information anyway). Have the servers ring in the bread & butter when they serve it. Then you can figure what these items cost per week, divided by the number of entrees served.

Either way, you will arrive at a semi-scientific number to use for your Wrap Around Cost. Let's imagine the Wrap Around is $2.00 per customer. You must add the $2.00 Wrap Around to the cost of every entrée to determine the real Cost of Goods.

Adding the Wrap Around Cost

Now let's take another look at the Sautéed Chicken Breast. As we previously determined, it cost $3.44 to produce the recipe plus $2 for the wrap around, the total cost to produce this dish is $3.44 + $2.00 = $5.44.

Now, let's take a second look at the sale price of our Sautéed Chicken Breast. $15 Price / $5.44 Cost = 35.6%, this is too high.

Because we know our food cost percentage goal is 32.1%, we can multiply $5.44 times 3 to show us what the cost would be at 33%. Then we can round the price up to find a fair price, for the owner and the customer.

Or, we could take $5.44 cost and divide it by .321 = $16.94, and round that up to $17. $5.44 divided by $17 = 32% with a $11.56 profit, not bad. We can also try it at $18 and $20. (see below).

I like to run a lower food cost % on the lower priced menu items like chicken, so I can get tighter on the higher priced items like steaks and seafood. It's OK to play around with different scenarios until you find the right mix for your business. Take a look at these pricing alternatives below.

Menu Item	$17.00 Price	$18.00 Price	$20.00 Price
Bronzed Chicken Breast	$3.44	$3.44	$3.44
Wrap Around Cost	$2.00	$2.00	$2.00
Total Cost of Menu Item	$5.44	$5.44	$5.44
Menu Price	$17.00	$18.00	$20.00
Food Cost %	32.0%	30.2%	27.2%
Profit Margin	$11.56	$12.56	$14.56

Food Cost Overview

We must do this cost exercise for every item on the menu. Then we put each menu item on a chart like the one below. The chart shows the cost to produce each item, the sale price of each item, as well as the cost percentage and profit margin for each menu item. We do this for every menu item, appetizers, salads, sides, entrees and desserts.

Menu Item	Cost	Price	%	Profit
Chicken	$5.34	$18.00	30.2%	$12.66
Hanger Steak	$10.74	$29.00	37.0%	$18.26
Salmon	$8.00	$26.00	30.7%	$18.00
Pasta	$6.00	$19.00	31.5%	$13.00
Shrimp	$7.00	$25.00	28.0%	$18.00
Totals	$37.08	$117.00	31.6%	$79.92
Averages	$7.41	$23.40	31.6%	$15.99

Think About This

Think back to our business plan, our average food and beverage check goal is $30.00 per person. We called for a 70/30 split of food and beverage (70% Food and 30% Bar).

This means our average food check must be at least $21 and our average bar check must be at least $9. In the example above the average entrée price is $23.40, slightly higher than our $21 goal.

When we add a drink or two to each guest check, we should be at or above our $30 average check goal. The calculations on the chart above show our food cost at 31.6%, which is slightly better than our 32% goal.

When we get real numbers (empirical data) from operations, we can make adjustments. We will also need to listen to feedback from our customers and employees. The trick is to find a pricing structure that works well for both the customer and the owner.

The Product Mix

The next step is the PRODUCT or MENU MIX REPORT. This report will come from your Point of Sales System. The product mix report will tell you how many of each item you actually sold during the period of measurement. It is important that the sales periods and the product mix period are exactly the same dates.

For Example: Week One January 1-7. The goal is to get the numbers from the Menu Mix Report to match the Numbers from your P&L Report.

Item	# Sold
Chicken	100
Hanger Steak	100
Salmon	60
Pasta	120
Shrimp	80
House Salad	50
Caesar Salad	100
Kale Salad	100
Flat Bread	100
Spinach Dip	75
Shrimp Cocktail	30
Key Lime Pie	40
Crème Brule	100

When you know how many of each item you have sold, you plug them into the Theoretical Food Cost Chart. The Theoretical Food Cost Chart shows:

- The number of each item sold
- The sales price of each item
- The total sales for each menu item
- The cost to produce each item
- The total cost for all items
- The food cost percentage
- The profit margins

Theoretical Food Cost Chart

The Theoretical Food Cost helps us know what your food cost should be in a Perfect World.

Food	# Sold	Sale Price	Total Sales	Item Cost	Total Cost	Food Cost	Profit Margin
ENTREES							
Chicken	100	$18	$1,800	$5.34	$534	29.6%	$1,266
Hanger Steak	100	$29	$2,900	$10.74	$1,074	37.0%	$1,826
Salmon	60	$26	$1,560	$8.00	$480	30.7%	$1,080
Pasta	120	$19	$2,280	$6.00	$720	31.5%	$1,560
Shrimp	80	$25	$2,000	$7.00	$560	28.0%	$1,440
SALADS							
House Salad	50	$6	$300	$1.50	$75	25.0%	$225
Caesar Salad	100	$8	$800	$1.60	$160	20.0%	$640
Kale Salad	100	$8	$800	$2.00	$200	25.0%	$600
APPETIZERS							
Flat Bread	100	$10	$1,000	$2.00	$200	20.0%	$800
Spinach Dip	75	$12	$900	$2.50	$188	20.8%	$712
Shrimp Cocktail	30	$12	$660	$5.00	$150	22.7%	$510
DESSERTS							
Key Lime Pie	40	$6	$240	$1.50	$60	25.0%	$180
Crème Brule	100	$8	$800	$1.20	$120	15.0%	$680
TOTALS	**1055**		**$ 16,040**		**$4,521**	**30.0%**	**$11,519**
# Guests Served			700				700
Avg Check/Profit			**$22.87**				**$16.45**

Food Cost Comparison

The Theoretical Food Cost Chart above shows how many of each menu item we sold and the sales total for each item.

It also shows we served 700 customers and should have an average food check of $22.87. It shows our Total Food Sales = $16,040 / Cost of Goods = $4,521 / Profit Margin = $11,519.

The next step is to compare the (THEORETICAL NUMBERS to the P&L NUMBERS for the same time period, to see if they match.

Category	P&L Report	Optimum Report
Sales	$16,500	$16,040
Food Purchases	$5,500	$4,521
Food Cost %	33.3%	30.0%
Profit Margin	**$11,000**	**$11,519**

Oops These Number Don't Match!

Imagine the Sales on the P&L are $16,500 and the Theoretical is $16,040. The sales don't match, neither does the food cost percentage. The goal is to get these numbers to match.

The first time you do this exercise there will be a BIG difference. As you work to tighten your record keeping and tighten your systems to get closer to Theoretical, the difference should shrink, and your food cost should improve!

You might be asking, "Why are the numbers different?" Few reasons:

- Bad Accounting
- Incorrect Recipe Costing
- Not Following the Recipe
- Bad Portioning
- Waste
- Theft
- Incorrect Prices
- and the greatest excuse of all time: Inventory Variance!

Now, it's time to move on to one of my favorite subjects…

Inventory

Inventory is an event that happens every week or every month in most restaurants. Inventory involves counting all your food and beverage items and multiplying them by what they cost to determine the dollar value of your food or bar inventory at a given time. We use the inventory to help calculate food and bar cost percentages.

Here's an example of how inventory works, in a weekly scenario: You start the week with Opening Inventory of $5,000. You purchase $3,300 in groceries. We add the Opening Inventory to the purchases which shows that you had a total of $8,300 in food available to use during the week.

To figure out your food cost for the week, we need to know how much money you really spent. So, we do a Closing Inventory. We recount all the food in the coolers and on the shelves. Then we multiply each item times what it cost to purchase them. This gives us a Closing Inventory is $5,000.

To arrive at our Cost of Goods. We subtract your Closing Inventory of $5,000 from the Total Food available $8,300 which give us a $3,300 Cost of Goods. Then we divide the Cost of Goods by Sales, and we see that our Food Cost Percentage is 33%. This is a perfect scenario. See the chart below.

	Inventory Example		
	Opening Inventory	$5,000	
+	Purchases	$3,300	
=	**Total**	**$8,300**	
-	Closing Inventory	$5,000	*No Inventory Variance*
=	**Cost of Goods**	**$3,300**	
/	Sales	$10,000	
=	**Food Cost Percentage**	**33%**	

In the example above, Opening Inventory and Closing Inventory are the same, there is no difference or variance. This is a very clean example. Our purchases equal our Cost of Goods.

There may be other considerations in your food cost, such as comps and promotions, that cloud the water, but for this discussion, we will keep it simple.

If your Closing Inventory is higher than $5,000, your food cost will be lower than 33% and if your Closing Inventory is lower than $5,000 your food cost will be higher than 33%. The biggest problem with inventory is that it is NEVER accurate.

Inventory has two parts:

1. Counting
2. Costing

Most Chefs and Managers don't do a good job counting or costing their inventory. They simply don't have time. The truth is Inventory is ALWAYS wrong, and it is a huge WASTE of time!

The Food Guru Says, "Stop Doing Inventory!"

It's the only way to stop the inventory variance excuse. I believe that inventory is a huge waste of time in 90% of independent restaurants, because it is never accurate. Inventory is usually just a gigantic exercise in fiction.

I know what you are saying, "Good businesses must do inventory." OK, fine. One time a year for your CPA and the IRS. The rest of the year forget about it.

I pay ACH for food because I want to, and pay COD for booze, because the law says I must. This helps us get the best prices and keeps us from getting behind with our prime vendors. When we receive the goods, we spend the money, both literally and from an accounting perspective. I charge PURCHASES against food cost and bar cost when it is PURCHASED.

I do not consider the inventory variance. The money has been spent, the food has been purchased, so it counts against cost. The chef and bar manager can worry about their stupid inventory variance.

I am in my restaurants every day. I see every invoice and I see what the inventory levels look like. I see purchase vs sales on the P&L every day. I use a Par Purchasing System, and I measure PURCHASES vs SALES.

Par Purchasing System

The Par Purchasing System replaces the need for inventory. We set a Par for every item that we use. If we use 100 pounds of chicken every week, we set PAR at 100#. If we use 10 cases of tomatoes every week, we set par at 10 cases. You get the idea.

131

We never have to guess how much of something we need. We just bring everything back to Par. Another way to say this is that we purchase ONLY what we used last week. Purchasing is simply REPLACING the inventory we used last week.

If your Sales are $10,000, and your cost of goods goal is 33%, you should use $3,300 worth of food. Your inventory should be reduced by $3,300. Your inventory should go from $5,000 - $3,300 = $1,700.

For Example:

- Sales $10,000 / Purchases $3,300 = Cost of Food 33%.
- If the chef spends $3,500, the food cost will be 35%. *($10,000 / $3,500 = 35%)*
- If he spends $4,000 our food cost will be 40%. *($10,000 / $4,000 = 40%)*

Simple to understand, right?

Think about it like this… You start the week with a $5,000 food inventory on Monday morning. From Monday – Sunday you have $10,000 in food sales. Your food purchases are $3,300. You must still have a $5,000 inventory for your food cost to be 33%. If you have less than $5,000 in food inventory your food cost will be HIGHER than 33%.

		Example #1	
	Opening Inventory	$5,000	
+	Purchases	$3,300	
=	**Total**	**$8,300**	
-	Closing Inventory	$5,000	No Inventory Variance
=	**Cost of Goods**	**$3,300**	
/	Sales	$10,000	
=	**Food Cost Percentage**	**33%**	

Now Hear This

If food inventory is not $5,000, you lose either way. If your closing inventory comes in at $5,500, instead of $5,000 that means you spent and extra $500 that should have gone to the bottom line as PROFIT.

We still have the groceries, but they are just dollars sitting on a shelf, instead of being in the bank where we can use them for other important things, such as payroll, or shoes for your kids.

	Example #2		
	Opening Inventory	$5,000	
+	Purchases	$3,800	
=	**Total**	**$8,800**	
-	Closing Inventory	$5,500	+ $500 Variance
=	**Cost of Goods**	**$3,300**	
/	Sales	$10,000	
=	**Food Cost Percentage**	**33%**	

If our purchases are 33% and our closing inventory comes in at $4,500, I'm really pissed because, we used (wasted) $500, which means we really ran a 38% Food Cost percentage and have no chance of recovering the lost cash.

	Example #3		
	Opening Inventory	$5,000	
+	Purchases	$3,300	
=	**Total**	**$8,300**	
-	Closing Inventory	$4,500	- $500 Variance
=	**Cost of Goods**	**$3,800**	
/	Sales	$10,000	
=	**Food Cost Percentage**	**38%**	

If closing inventory is only $4,500, that is $500 lower than the $5,000 we started the week with (we have to add the $500 to purchases) which makes the cost of goods $3,300 + the $500 inventory variance. Our cost of food is the $3,300 in purchases plus the $500 reduction from inventory = $3,800.

Our food cost is now $3,800 / $10,000 = .38% or 5% too high or $500 right out of my pocket! No shoes for you!

It has been my experience that the Chef or Manager will always have some lame excuse as to why purchases were high. They will say they had to buy lobster this week or we had a prime rib banquet, or we have two new cooks, the story goes on and on, blah, blah, blah. This process is a never-ending battle between the Owner and the Chef. The best way to end the battle is to STOP DOING INVENTORY!

Simply divide Purchases into Sales and get a percentage. If purchases are high, food cost is high, plain and simple. If I have to write a check, the money has been spent. So that means it counts against food cost.

This also saves the Chef and Managers the time of counting stuff and extending (bogus) inventory reports. Managers can use this extra time to train, cut production dollars and increase sales. It's a Win/Win/Win.

The point is that every dollar you allow your Chef or Bar Manager to spend comes out of YOUR pocket. I'd rather have the cash in the bank instead of lame excuses and excess inventory. The process is exactly the same for all Cost of Goods: Food, Bar and even t-shirts, souvenirs, and trinkets.

Bar Costing Example

Bar costing works the same exact way as food costing. We must cost every beer, glass of wine, bottle of wine, mixed drink and cocktail. Our bar cost goal is lower than our food cost goal, in the bar we aim for 25% or less. Here are the percentages that I aim for in each bar category:

Product or Category	Cost
Cocktails	15-20%
Domestic Beer	25-30%
Craft or Specialty Beer	20-25%
Wine by the Glass	20-25%
Wine by the Bottle - $25-$50	25-30%
Wine by the Bottle - 50-$100	30-33%
Wines by the Bottle - over $100	33-40%

Costing a Drink

The example below shows a Lemon Drop martini with two different price examples to see what happens at a $7 price and an $9 price. Personally, I like the $9 price.

Remember our goal is to run a 25% overall Bar Cost. The Cost of Goods on Cocktails should be between 15-20%.

Lemon Drop Martini	Example #1	Example #2
Citron Vodka	$1.00	$1.00
Fresh Lemon Juice	$0.30	$0.30
Simple Syrup	$0.15	$0.15
Garnish	$0.05	$0.05
Total Cost	$1.50	$1.50
Sales Price	**$7.00**	**$9.00**
Cost %	21.4%	16.6%
Profit Margin	**$5.50**	**$7.50**

Product	Cost	Price	%	Margin
Domestic Beer	$0.80	$3.50	23.0%	$2.70
Specialty Beer	$1.25	$5.00	25.0%	$3.75
Wine by the Glass	$1.50	$7.00	21.0%	$5.50
Wine by the Bottle	$10.00	$33.00	30.0%	$23.00
Mixed Drink	$1.00	$6.00	16.6%	$5.00
Specialty Cocktail	$1.50	$10.00	15.0%	$8.50
Totals	**$16.05**	**$64.50**	**24.8%**	**$48.45**
Average per menu item		**$6.78**		**$5.35**

Our percentages in the Bar Cost Overview above look like they will fall in line with our goals, but we will need to see what happens with operations and sales mix. Then we will make adjustments.

Note: I cut the bottle of wine in half, assuming that two people will be drinking it, which gives us an average drink check average of $6.78, right in-line with our budget:

- $30 average check
- $24 food
- $6 for the bar

Now that we know what our cost per serving is supposed to be, we must train our staff to use jiggers and make each drink with the correct amount of each ingredient, every time.

We do this for cost and consistency. Remember, the goal is to deliver a consistent experience every time. To accomplish this, our drinks must be made consistently!

The Bar Menu Cost Overview

You should be able to run a report on your Point of Sale that will tell you how many of each menu item you sold during the measurement period. Then, you can use this information to determine your THEORETICAL Cost of Goods for the bar, just like we did with the food cost.

Product	# Sold	Cost	Total	Price	Total	%	Profit
Domestic Beer	100	$0.80	$80	$3.50	$350	23%	$270
Specialty Beer	100	$1.25	$125	$5.00	$500	25%	$375
Glass Wine	100	$1.50	$150	$7.00	$700	21%	$550
Wine Bottle	50	$8.00	$400	$30.00	$1,500	27%	$1,100
Mixed Drink	100	$1.25	$125	$8.00	$800	16%	$675
Specialty Cocktail	200	$1.50	$300	$12.00	$2,400	13%	$2,100
Totals	**650**		**$1,200**		**$6,250**	**20%**	**$5,050**
Average per menu item					**$6.78**		**$5.35**

I hope you get the idea. The goal is to get and keep your cost of goods in line with the budget. Getting your numbers right will take serious time and effort.

I believe this process will help you achieve your bottom-line goals. Don't be afraid to contact me if you need help with this. My email address is foodguru@foodguru.com. Let's move on to another one of my favorite subjects: Labor Costs.

Labor Cost

The process I am about to show you will help you see the big picture and make the tough decisions regarding your schedule and labor dollars.

Remember, you are not here for a popularity contest; you are here to build a great restaurant and that includes balancing the basic fundamentals AND earning a profit.

Don't be a Coward!

A good manager must be able to write an effective schedule that fits the budget every week. Controlling labor cost is much harder than controlling cost of goods because of the human element.

Most owners and managers like their employees and want to see them earn enough money to pay their bills, support their family and enjoy life. Personally, I like the employees who are the most productive and do the best job for the business and the customer. I reward the best people with the best money, hours and shifts and replace under-performers, as fast as possible.

What Is Our Labor Budget?

Remember the 30-30-30-10? That means our labor cost should equal 30% of our sales. To determine what our labor cost should be, we divide annual sales by 52 weeks and multiply that number by .30%.

Example: Sales $1,000,000 / 52 weeks = $19,230 per week x .30% = $5,769. This is what we can spend per week on <u>LABOR COST</u> and <u>PAYROLL TAXES</u> and achieve a 30% labor cost.

The next question: Is $5,769 a fair and reasonable number? To determine if this is a reasonable amount, we create what I call a linear schedule.

The Linear Schedule

This is the tool we use to help us determine what our schedule should be. The Linear Schedule will help you write a schedule that fits your budget. The Linear Schedule, schedules POSITIONS, not people. It takes the mystery out of the scheduling process.

To start the process, you will meet with your department managers and build a Liner Schedule. This exercise will spark some fun conversation and be a real eye opener for everybody.

Here are the steps:

1. Decide what POSITIONS (cooks, waiters and bartenders and managers) you need in order to accomplish the tasks and deliver the Customer Promise.
2. Determine what TASKS need to be accomplished before, during, and after service?
3. Create an exact CHECKLIST for each position, with time limits for each task.
4. Determine what time each cook, waiter, and bartender should start work.
5. Determine what time each position should finish.
6. Determine the market rate for each position?
7. Determine how you will pay each position?

The concept is similar to writing a schedule. You list the positions, the amount of hours per day and week then cost it out. This process focuses on the needs of the business and gives the owner, managers, and employees solid information regarding the schedule.

Once you determine what each position should be, what each position should do, and how much you are willing to pay each position; you can recruit people to play the positions. The Linear schedule is the perfect tool to help you write an effective schedule.

Six Days Per Week

Lunear Schedule

AM Position	9a	10a	11a	12p	1p	2p	3p	Hours	Rate	Total $
Manager	x	x	x	x	x	x	x	8	$15	$120
Cook #1	x	x	x	x	x	x	x	7	$10	$70
Cook #2	x	x	x	x	x	x	x	7	$10	$70
Waiter #1		x	x	x	x	x	x	6	$5	$30
Waiter #2		x	x	x	x	x	x	6	$5	$30
Total AM								**38**		**$420**

PM Position	3p	4p	5p	6p	8p	9p	10p	Hours	Rate	Total $
Manager	x	x	x	x	x	x	x	8	$15	$120
Grille	x	x	x	x	x	x	x	8	$12	$96
Sauté		x	x	x	x	x	x	7	$12	$84
Pantry		x	x	x	x	x	x	7	$10	$70
Dish/Prep			x	x	x	x	x	6	$10	$60
Waiter #1		x	x	x	x	x	x	7	$5	$28
Waiter #2		x	x	x	x	x	x	7	$5	$35
Waiter #3			x	x	x	x		4	$5	$20
Bartender	x	x	x	x	x	x	x	8	$8	$64
Total PM								**62**		**$577**

Daily Labor $	$997
Weekly Labor $	$5,982
Payroll Taxes	$600
Total Labor	**$6,582**
Sales	$19,230
Labor %	34.2%

A small restaurant can't afford to pay the managers to sit in the office. Everyone must have a working role. In the example above, the AM Manager is the General Manager. The GM does the daily paperwork and works as lunch host and floor manager. The PM Manager is the PM host and floor manager.

In the example above, our schedule cost is $5,982 plus, $600 in payroll taxes = $6,582. Divide that by sales of $19,230 = 34.2% Labor Cost.

Let's see how this compares to the budget: Our Sales goal is $19,230. Our Labor Budget is .30% of Sales = $5,769. Our linear schedule is $813 above our budget! We need to cut $813 from our schedule to get down to our 30% budget.

A Real-World Conundrum

As the owner of this business, what would you do to get your numbers in line? I see three alternatives:

1. We can cut staff
2. We can increase sales, or a combination of both.
3. We can lower cost of goods or other cost, to get us closer to the 30/30/30/10.

Option #1 Cut Staff

We can bring someone in later or send them home earlier. Maybe we can eliminate a person on the slower days of the week? Maybe we can lower the hourly rate? I have several issues with these ideas.

- **Issue #1:** We don't want to cut staff and allow our standards to slip. If we allow this to happen, we begin the process of saving ourselves out of business.
- **Issue #2:** We often say we are going to send people home early, but it rarely happens.
- **Issue #3:** If we lower the pay rate, make sure that it is only for the weakest people. If you take money away from your stars, they will quit, and you will be screwed.

Remember earlier in the book when we said that labor is a Fixed Cost? The linear schedule is supposed to be the minimum that we need, so we can't reduce it, without serious consequences. That's why it's fixed.

Option #2 Keep the Staff

This is the easiest and may be smartest thing we can do, for two reasons:

- **Reason #1:** The goal of business is to increase sales and grow. It is possible and desirable to grow your sales to fit the fixed staff requirements. If you increase sales by 10% to $21,600, your labor cost percentage will come down to 30%.

- **Reason #2:** Sometimes we need to run higher cost in one category than the others. Perhaps you can run a lower cost of goods and/or other cost to make up for the higher labor cost.

The linear schedule will give you some good points to ponder. If your labor cost is higher than 30% and your profit is less than 10%, you need to do some thinking.

The theme of this chapter is "Manage the Money". To do this you must Squeeze Expenses & Increase Yield. This brings us to the next question, "How can we get more out of each position?"

Time Management / Increase Yield

Time is the great equalizer, nothing else on earth is equal. Some people have more money, more brains, more talent; some have better health, connections and opportunity.

Time is the only thing on earth that we all have the same amount of. We all have 24 hours in a day, seven days a week, 365 days a year. It is how we spend our time that makes the difference.

I will bet that you think you are working too hard, and that you feel there is never enough time in a day to get all the things you have to do, done. I will also bet that your managers and employees feel the same way.

I hate to break your heart but, I believe that you and your staff are only working at 50% of your true potential. I really believe you can *DOUBLE* your production!

I'll bet that your people stand around in your (dirty) restaurant talking (smack) about how unfair you are, and how much "this place sucks". I'll further bet that 95% of you will think I'm wrong, and you will do NOTHING to change your situation. Denial is expensive, very expensive.

Let's start with an easy one to get us on the same page. I think we can all agree that there are times during every shift when it's slow and there are other times when it's crazy busy. It's the natural flow in most restaurants.

If you want to achieve the 30-30-30-10 and make money, you must train your people to fill the slow times with important work. This will help to make the crazy times a little easier and might help you save thousands of dollars every year.

STOP!

I want to insert a very important point for you to think about: This is a distraction for my point, but it is mission critical, so here it is: If you have the same SLOW times every day and your people are all standing around hating life and getting into trouble, why are you open at those times?

Let's take Mids for example (the time between lunch and dinner). Who told you that you had to be open during Mids? And, why are you open during those hours if they only drain energy and cost you money? Personally, I closed during MIDS about three years ago, and everybody's mental health has improved and by the way, so has my bank account. We used to have days where the labor cost was higher than sales. Closing for Mids lowered my labor cost and made my people happier. It's a Win, Win, Win!

The other thing about Mids is we often discount our prices during those hours to bring people in, which causes a double whammy of wasted time and devaluing the product. The same thing goes for Happy Hour. If you have to drastically reduce prices to get people in the restaurant, and you are NOT making money… Why the #@^& are you even open? I believe it is smarter to adjust your hours to fit your business, than to game the system with deals and discounts. Just a thought, now back to our topic…

In America, most people are paid an hourly wage because our government requires it. You must teach your people that TIME is VALUABLE, and they must maximize their production. You must stop paying your employees to stand around and bitch. You must hire and keep the people who have a positive attitude and get important things done! Teach them to play Pac Man instead of bitching and texting. (Or, change your schedule of when you're open.)

Your employee's motivation is to get paid $15 for every hour they are physically at work. However, your motivation is to get productive work done while paying your employees by the hour.

Standing around chit-chatting is NOT productive. Texting is NOT productive. Smoke breaks are NOT productive. The next time you see one of your people standing around doing nothing, while they are on the clock, send them home. If you think that idea is too radical… *fire them! -Whoa!*

Time is Money!

Restaurants that have high labor cost (above 33%) have serious time management problems. Time management is like a game show, there must be a time limit for every task.

Check out Frederick Taylor, the world's first efficiency expert. Google "Taylorism Video" and watch a few videos. You'll get the idea.

Warning: *Frederick Taylor is a radical dangerous thinker who you will love. He was the guy who taught Henry Ford about the assembly line. The problem is that the liberal "feel good" police hate Frederick Taylor because he represents old school, outdated thinking. Personally, I love old school outdated thinking! Especially stuff like hard work, integrity, and discipline. I believe it gives me an edge over the modern self-entitlement and socialism for all folks.*

I guarantee you can increase your production and reduce your labor cost by 10%, starting today.

Who is a better time manager, the chef or the newest cook? The answer better be the chef! The point is, the Chef should be teaching the newest cook how to best perform each task and manage their time to get the most work done during their shift.

As the government imposed minimum wage goes UP and UP, it will become much harder for us to employ slackers. At $10 per hour you can slack off at a factor of 10. At $15, you can only slack off at a factor of 5. At $20, you can't slack off. Time is Valuable, Time is Money!

Play Pacman

The goal of Pac Man is to move around the screen eating stuff and earning points. There are even bonus points for eating special stuff. It should be the same thing in your restaurant.

Your employees should be doing as much as possible to earn as many points as possible. The more points they earn, the more money they should be paid. Reward the people who produce the best results. Fire the people who suck the clock. *Fire the Clocksuckers!*

Caution!

Having too many people is a big problem, it can be worse than not having enough people. Most restaurant operators are used to struggling to find enough good people to fill all the positions. When we have too many good people, we are afraid to cut staff to the point that we actually need, because we believe (know) someone will quit, and we will be short-handed, yet again.

Too Many People

Two things happen when you have too many people, and both are bad:

1. High Labor Cost
2. High Drama

If you are spending 10% or more time on drama (employee or management squabbles), you have too many people on the schedule. You must terminate the drama queens. Or, as we just discussed, change your hours of operation, to fit your business.

Eliminate Grunge

The key to good time management is to eliminate wasted steps (grunge) from the process and focus only on the things that are mission critical. Look at your USP (Unique Selling Proposition) keep the IMPORTANT steps and procedures that help you Deliver the Customer Promise and eliminate the ones that don't. Think back to our Cheeseburger Restaurant example.

Break out the Stop Watch

Management must get involved in setting production standards. Management must set time limits for each and every task. You must get your people focused and moving.

Hey... did you watch those Frederick Taylor videos I told you about yet? Whenever you watch them, send me a quick email about your thoughts, I'd love to hear from you.

Restaurant Set-Up, Operating, and Closing Duties are the same every day. Everyone should know exactly what they are supposed to do in order to get their station ready for the shift. There is no mystery involved... it's the same thing every single day.

Every employee/position must have a printed checklist with each duty to be performed (including time limits).

- Each employee must check off the items as they are completed.
- Each employee must SIGN the completed checklist.
- The manager or shift leader must inspect and sign the checklist.
- The checklist must be turned in to the office... every day!

Discipline

If the employee or manager checks off tasks that were not completed, they must be disciplined.

1. First Offense – Written Warning
2. Second Offense – Screaming & Written Warning
3. Third Offense – You're Fired (No Screaming Required)

I find screaming to have therapeutic value. I'd rather get it off my chest now, than carry it around and have a heart attack later!

Having said that, I would like to add, when you find yourself screaming at the same #@^*head over and over again, just fire them. It will be better for everybody in the long run, even the #@^*head.

The Best

I have noticed that the best cooks come into the kitchen, wash their hands and start cutting stuff up. I have also noticed that the best bartenders are behind the bar, in a crisp clean uniform organizing things 10 minutes before they are scheduled. The best waiters are in their stations getting things ready for service when they are scheduled. This is what we are looking for.

Micro-Tasks

"Restaurant-ing", is a game of seconds. Wasted seconds become wasted minutes and then wasted hours. In the kitchen, a good cook will drop a burger and an order of fries and then find ten micro-tasks to do during the 3 minutes it takes to cook the burger and fries. They don't stand there like a schmohawk watching the fries cook. The key to great time management is filling the seconds between tasks with many, many micro-tasks.

Oh, by the way… this applies double to MANAGERS.

I believe that most restaurant managers are just babysitters, who rarely get any important work done. They are great at complaining that they are overworked and underpaid, but if you paid them for performance only, they would be broke.

When it comes to managers, I believe talk is cheap. I measure my managers based on performance, not the amount of hours they work. Also, most of my managers get paid by the hour. This is the best and most fair way to do it. If they have to cover shifts and work tons of overtime – they get paid. If they want extra time off – they don't get paid. I find this to be a Win/Win/Win deal for everybody.

Food Guru Prediction

I predict that by the year 2025, 50% of the positions that exist in the restaurant industry today will be gone! They will be replaced by technology and/or a more effective workforce. I believe that we are just at the beginning stages of the technology explosion.

If you are interested in exploring this concept further, check out my Build a Better Restaurant Podcast, specifically the episode called "50% of All Restaurant Jobs Will Be Gone by 2025!"

Now we are heading toward the end of this exciting chapter, it's time to move on to Other Costs.

Other Costs

This refers to everything else you spend money on. Other Costs are always considered Fixed Costs. There are two types of Other Costs.

- **Fixed Other Costs:** These are things like rent or mortgage, utilities and credit card fees. These things are negotiated before the restaurant opens for business and are difficult to change, after you are open.
- **Flexible Other Costs:** These line items are flexible and fairly easy to change. You can manage these items intelligently or allow your people to waste them with reckless abandon, the choice is up to you.

Other Cost - Fixed	
Rent / Mortgage	$60,000
Utilities	$20,000
Insurance	$12,000
Credit Card Fees (2% of sales)	$20,000
Trash Removal	$2,000

Other Cost - Variable	
Legal/ CPA	$6,000
Restaurant Supplies / Disposables	$30,000
Cleaning Supplies	$14,000
Linen & Laundry	$15,000
Office Supplies	$6,000
Repairs & Maintenance	$10,000
Sales & Marketing	$35,000
Comp Expense	$70,000

Total Other Cost (Fixed & Variable)	$300,000

Zero Overhead Growth

Other Cost & Labor Cost are sometimes called "Overhead". The key to success, is to keep your Overhead from growing. This means when you find the correct level for Labor Cost and Other Cost you must freeze it!

It's called Zero Overhead Growth! We must take a blood oath, to Zero Overhead Growth!

Here's what you do. Meet with your key managers every month and go over every single line item of your P&L. Go through every single invoice if you have to and ask these questions:

- What is this for?
- Why do we need this?
- Is this Mission Critical or Grunge?
- How can we do this thing, or buy this thing smarter and more effectively? I'm not talking about compromising quality and buying cheap crap, I'm taking about buying smarter.
- How can we improve production without increasing our current labor budget?
- How can we squeeze waste from our labor cost? Not by lowering wages, but by scheduling smarter. Sometimes, a higher hourly wage improves production.
- How can we squeeze waste from linen, cleaning supplies, disposable supplies and office supplies, without compromising our standards?
- How can we lower our electric, water or gas bill?

The goal is to keep the muscle and lose the fat. Fat is flagrant waste that doesn't improve the customer experience or move us toward any of our goals.

When you hit a sticking point, and your manager is arguing to keep something, ask them these questions.

- Are you willing to pay for this out of your own pocket?
- What about if I gave you 50% of this savings, how would you feel about it then?

Here's another idea. Have a meeting with every supplier that you buy from, ask these questions:

- How can we buy smarter and more effectively?
- How can you help us reduce cost and eliminate waste?
- What other products or services do you offer that could save us time and money?

Make sure that they understand that you are not trying to be cheap and demanding a price reduction, this never works, because we all have to make a living. I'm talking about finding areas where our suppliers can help us buy smarter and increase value to our customers. This must be another Win/Win/Win situation, for us, the vendor and the customer.

You will improve your business by SQUEEZING and GROWING. The key to improving the bottom line is to squeeze waste from your costs and grow your top line sales!

Don't "Save" Yourself Out of Business

Don't Save Yourself Out of Business. I love this one. You will never save yourself to wealth in the restaurant business. Never get so fixated on saving that you forget about selling! Vigorous sales cover sins.

The goal is to find ways to reduce waste and become more efficient and effective. This requires analytical thinking, time and lots of training.

You can improve your cost of goods. You can improve employee production and efficiency. You can freeze your overhead where it is today.

Then, you can focus on improving sales, improving food quality, and improving the customer experience. When you focus on these Basic Fundamentals, amazing things will happen. Remember: Z.O.G... zero overhead growth!

The BEST way to lower your cost percentages is to increase sales! *Vigorous sales cover sins!* Your goal is to maintain expenses at the current level and increase sales! You have to hold your people accountable and, they must hit the numbers!

"Money talks. Bullshit takes the bus."

    - Jordan Belfort, The Wolf of Wall Street

Personal Wealth & Financial Independence

Believe it or not, the real goal of owning a restaurant, or working for a living is to create Personal Wealth & Financial Independence.

Creating culinary masterpieces and fancy cocktails is a worthy occupation, but that's exactly what it is... it is an occupation, a craft. It's what we DO for a living.

As we discussed in the First Fundamental, the world wants you to be rich, so you can live the life of your dreams and enrich the lives of others. You are way too smart to settle for a life of "just scraping by".

There are two ways for you to create wealth:

1. Build your business to be SOLD later...
   Aggressive Investment
2. Build a personal retirement account...
   Passive Investment

If you own a restaurant, or any business, your chances for a great retirement go up significantly. On the flip side, your risk of failure is EXTREMELY HIGH, so you better have a great business system. Most of us got into the restaurant business to create great food and drinks. We didn't think of it as a long-term wealth generating machine. The beautiful things is that as a restaurant owner, you get to do BOTH.

People who work for other people, must create investments outside of their job, to build wealth. But for you, your restaurant is the place where you practice your craft AND create wealth! Financial Independence happens when your business becomes self-sufficient and you do not require assistance from other people or entities.

Financial Independence happens when your restaurant can pay you to do as you please. This means you have competent people managing your business and sending you a check every month.

You must design your restaurant in such a way, that it can produce a 10% PROFIT and be managed by average human beings with average business and culinary skills.

The goal is to build a "money making system" so your restaurant becomes an ATM that spits out cash every month! Remember, the goal is to build a business that can be sold in the future. You are building a business, not a demanding job! Nobody wants to buy a demanding job.

Your JOB is to build a business that makes MONEY! A business that someone will PAY lots of money to own when you are ready to retire and cash out. The point of this book is to help you build a restaurant operating system, that you can sell in the future.

Your 75-Year Old Self

Let's spend a few minutes talking about the 75-year old version of you. I imagine that you will want to retire at some time in the future. It is important to put some money aside for your future self. I use age 75, because I truly believe that 65 is way too young to retire--especially if you own the business and are doing something you love. 65 may be a great time to cut back and slow down, but it's way too young to retire.

I believe if you are under the age of 50 today, you will live to be 90 or even 100. You will need something constructive and fun to do. 65 is the "fourth quarter" of the game, many exciting things happen in the fourth quarter.

Now hear this: Your 75-year old self wants to have enough money, so they can live in a nice house, have good food, and decent medical care. Your 75-year old self wants to enjoy life, visit kids and grandkids from time to time, and maybe even do some traveling.

Please don't allow the 20-, 30-, 40-, 50- or 60-year old version of yourself to force your 75- or 85-year old self into POVERTY! You must save some real money for your retirement.

Every dollar that you piss away today could be $10+ that your 75-year old self will NOT have. Every dollar that you SAVE today, can become $10 your 75-year old self WILL have, if you play your financial cards well.

Imagine that you put $200 each month into a retirement account starting at age 25. That's only $50 a week, if you work full time as a waiter, cook or manager in decent restaurant, you should be able to do that easily. If you work a little overtime, investing $200 a month should be easy.

$200 each month x 12 Months = $2,400 per year. After ten years, by your 35th birthday, you should have $24,000.

If you earn a 7% return, your money will double every 10 years. It's called "The Power of 72". Take the number 72, divide it by the interest rate, and it will tell you how long it takes to double the amount. That means money at 6% will double every 12 years, money invested at 7% doubles about every 10 years, and money invested at 10%, will double every 7 years.

Saving money comes down to your philosophy. Rich people SAVE first and spend what's left. Poor people SPEND first and save what's left. You cannot change the past, but you can change your philosophy going forward?

Remember, when it comes to money, the earlier you get started, the more time your money will have to grow! *It's time to giddy up!*

Chapter Recap

The key concepts in this chapter are:

- Sales Must Be 10% Greater Than Expenses
- 86% Of Restaurants Don't See Their 5th Birthday
- As You Think – So Shall You Be
- The Goal Of The P&L Statement Is 30-30-30-10
- Cost Every Menu Item
- Stop Doing Inventory
- Time Is Money
- Control Labor Cost With The Linear Schedule
- Z.O.G. Zero Overhead Growth
- Don't Save Yourself Out Of Business
- Build Personal Wealth – Take Care Of Your 75-Year Old Self

Take a minute and write down your personal retirement plan. Your 75-year old self is curious and wants to know where they are going to live, and how much money they will have to spend on FUN!

My Personal Retirement Plan is:

My 75-years old self will have $_____ in the bank.

While the ideas in this chapter are still fresh in your mind. I want you to make a list of 10 ways you can improve the way you manage your money.

Fundamental #7:
Build a Bullet-Proof Operating System

It is time to pull all the previous chapters together into an Operating System. This is the Who, What, Where, When & How of your restaurant. Your System will liberate you from "restaurant owner bondage" and allow you to live the life of your dreams.

The System

Let me ask you a few opening questions:

- Can you take two weeks off without your restaurant falling apart?
- Do you have recipes & pictures for every menu item?
- Do you have qualified people in every position?
- Do your employees have checklists to follow?
- Do your managers have checklists to follow?
- Do they follow them?
- Are you sure?
- Really?

Imagine, it's 4:45 in the afternoon, and your restaurant is about to open at 5:00. Are your people prepared, poised, and ready? Or are they sloppy, confused, and disorganized? Are your waiters still in street clothes talking about the big party last night, or are they sharply dressed in crisp uniforms, putting the finishing touches on their tables? Are your cooks out back smoking cigarettes, or are they fine-tuning their station?

The difference between success and failure comes down to being Prepared, Poised & Ready Vs. Disorganized, Confused & Sloppy.

"Every battle is won or lost before it is ever fought."

- Sun Tzu, The Art of War

The System is the Who, What, Where, When, and How of your business. The Universe is the best example of how a great and powerful system works. A rose seed will grow into a perfect and beautiful rose every time, provided that it has adequate sun, water, nutrients, and temperature.

Your restaurant also has a system and it is defined by everything your people do, from the way they sweep the floor, to the way they plate each entrée and serve it to your guests. The better the system, the better the restaurant.

There are three ways to do things:

1. The Right Way
2. The Wrong Way
3. The Only Way

The Right Way

The system documents the right way to do things, the performance standards, the exact details, procedures, checklists and recipes for how everything should be de done. The goal of the system is to teach managers and employees how to do everything the right way.

The system is the answer book, it explains how we do it here. Restaurants without a well-documented and trainable system lose the game before it starts.

There are two parts of a system:

1. The TRIBAL METHOD is when we have a senior staff member show the new people how to do the work.
2. The WRITTEN SYSTEM consists of neatly typed manuals with pictures and sometimes video or PowerPoint presentations.

The Wrong Way

The wrong way is the exact opposite of the right way, it happens when someone deviates from the system, due to ignorance, laziness or sloth (I love that word – sloth).

The next time you see one of your people doing something the wrong way, ask yourself, "Is this thing that they are doing the wrong way *their* fault, or a weakness in the system?"

The truth is, your people are operating the system exactly the way you have taught them to. Your people are operating to your current level of expectations. So if you are not happy with the performance of your team, you must upgrade the system and raise the standards.

150

The only way is like a Band-Aid. It happens when something goes wrong, like when the internet goes down. The only way will get you from here to there, but it should only be used in emergency situations.

Upgrades

Here is a great way to look at your restaurant: Instead of thinking that you have made many, many mistakes, look at them as things that need to be "upgraded".

This happens every day at places like Microsoft and Apple. They release a product or software that still has a few bugs or kinks that need to be worked out or finished. Then, they send out the upgrades to fix the bugs and make their product work better as they create them.

Think of your operating system as version 1.0, 2.0, 3.0, and so on. Times change, new information surfaces, we learn as we go; and if you want to improve, you must be constantly tweaking, fixing, and upgrading the system.

The Human Element

There will always be slight differences and variations between the way we want things to be done, and the way our people actually do them. This is because of the human element.

Each person on the team has a different level or talent, ability and viewpoint, we all come from different backgrounds and see things differently.

Think of the difference between people and computers:

- **Computers** are far more accurate than humans. This is because computers are based on binary code, ones and zeros, just like 2+2 will always equal 4. Computers will do things exactly the same way every time, that is how they are programmed.
- **Humans** do everything differently... every single time. Just like snowflakes, no two are alike.

Here's an example: If two people roll 100 spring rolls, every single one will be slightly different, compare that to manufacturing 100,000 iPhones.

Simple & Complex

There are simple systems and complex systems. Systems that work always start out simple and then, as the business evolves and grows, more layers of complexity are added. McDonalds is a great example of this, they started with a simple system in 1954, and today their system us ultra-complex.

"Any intelligent fool can make things bigger, more complex, and more violent. It takes a touch of genius—and a lot of courage to move in the opposite direction."

- E.F. Schumacher

Eliminate "Grunge"

There is a big difference between complex and grunge. Grunge is the excess stuff you have laying around your restaurant. Grunge is the excess steps built into your systems and procedures. Grunge is the unnecessary items on your menu.

Grunge gets in the way and slows you and your business down. Grunge is the enemy of a smooth system. Let's revisit our burger joint example that serves 3 menu items, one size of each:

1. Cheeseburger
2. Fries
3. Coke (12 oz. can, no cups)

Because there are only three menu items to focus on, this system should be fast, clean and efficient. Think about how smooth your restaurant would run if you eliminated half the menu items and only focused on your core items. Remember the old adage, K.I.S.S. (Keep It Short & Simple).

Now, let's see how quickly "THEY" can screw up our simple menu. Let's add some things to the menu that "THEY" think we *must* have:

- Fountain Soda (five flavors, three sizes of cups, straws, lids)
- Chicken Sandwich
- Veggie Sandwich
- A variety of flavored buns for each sandwich
- Green Salad (four dressings)
- And why not add a grilled chicken salad & a fruit salad
- How about two sizes of fries
- And why not truffle fries & garlic fries

This is the kind of thinking that is killing places like McDonalds...

An Outsider's Point of View

Spend an entire day looking at your restaurant from an outsider's view point. Think of yourself as a fly on the wall. Watch your people do their jobs. Watch your customers as they experience your restaurant.

Study your product sales mix to see what is selling and what is not. Make a list of unnecessary steps in the process that don't line up with your core concept or help you deliver the Customer Promise. Then, sit down with your staff (the people who actually do the work), and ask if they have any ideas that could eliminate grunge & improve the process.

Listen carefully and take their ideas seriously. Your people can help you if you are open minded and willing to listen. Institute the ideas that make sense. Repeat the process every month. This is called "innovation".

Technology

I love technology! I was the first chef to podcast a video way back in 2005, so I understand and love technology. But technology is a great example of grunge. Think of all the computers, networks, routers, modems, printers and point of sale tools you have in your restaurant. Then add the music and multiple TV systems, then add email, text, Twitter, Facebook, Instagram and whatever else comes next.

Think of all the time you spend trying to figure out and fix simple computer and technology related problems. I ask you: "Who has time to focus on great food and drinks and taking care of the guests?"

Think of how much time your managers and employees spend on their phones, while there are customers in the restaurant. This is GRUNGE! Grunge is the enemy of great performance. Think how much more productive your people could be if they would put down their damn phones and do their jobs.

Training

New employees are created by both, growth and turnover.

Either way, every employee has to start at the beginning, just like a new baby. Every new employee has to flounder around for a while, trying to figure things out. This requires a huge investment of time and money.

You must create a system to train people quickly. A good system uses two types of training methods.

1. The Tribal Method
2. The Written System

The Tribal Method

This is when a manager or trainer uses "Show & Tell", to train new people. In the dining room, we show them how to polish silverware, roll napkins and set tables. We teach them the table numbers, and how to greet a table. This is the most common way to train people, however; it is fraught with error because every trainer, teaches things differently.

The Written System

These are printed manuals, PowerPoint slides & video tutorials. This is usually much better. These materials are great for things that rarely change.

Food & Drink Recipes and Job Duty Checklists fit nicely in this category. But the exact nuance of greeting a table and upselling are often better with the Tribal Method.

Also, I love using SCRIPTS to teach waiters and service people how to answer the phone and greet tables. Scripts lay out the basic, most important information from start to finish. After using the script for a while, a good waiter can (and should) be able to add their own personal twist, ABOVE the minimum standard, provided that they meet or hopefully exceed the required results. But don't change for the sake of change, this only creates confusion.

YouTube Videos

Here's another thought on training: The next time you hire a server who doesn't know how to open a bottle of wine, tell them to go on the internet and watch a few videos.

Then, have them open one in front of the dining room staff the next day. This will show you their capacity to learn on their own. Remember, we need SELF-STARTERS! Self-Starters find a way to WIN!

You don't need to reinvent the wheel. You need to use the tools and resources that are available. One of my managers replaced some kitchen floor tiles, after watching a few YouTube videos and saved us lots of money! YouTube Videos are a great resource – Use them!

Work On (Not In) The Business

The role of the owner is to create the vision, the mission, the goal. The owner must do the big picture thinking of the entrepreneur or CEO and leave the operational duties to the managers and employees. When the owner is buried in the operational work, there is no leader at the helm, nobody driving the bus.

I understand that every restaurant is different, and some owners work as the chef, bartender, or maître d' as well as the accountant. I work my ass off every day. I also understand that one of the biggest mistakes an owner can make is, trying to wear too many different hats at the same time.

The Four Different Mindsets

This is good stuff that I got from Michael Gerber, who got it from Peter Drucker, so pay attention!

The Technician

The technician is the part of us that loves the rush of a busy shift. We love to work the line, expedite, seat guests, bus tables, make drinks and wash dishes. These are the reasons why we got into the restaurant business to begin with.

While we are doing these tasks, we realize how much fun they are, and we also remember that nobody else can do it quite as well as we do! It's true, I'm a GREAT dishwasher and busboy!

The Artist

The artist is the creative part of us. The Artists loves to create new drinks and dishes for the customer to experience. The artist needs their ego stroked on a regular basis. The artist thinks system are for places like the Olive Garden.

The artist is convinced that the solution to every problem is more cutting-edge food and drink. The artist is convinced that the system is holding them back from reaching their creative potential.

The artist avoids the business side of the equation, because it's too black and white. The solution to this is, don't expect artists to be managers, let the artists to be artists, and hire managers to manage the business.

The Manager

The manager is the organized part of us that labels the cooler and the storeroom. The manager also creates the job checklists, financial spreadsheets and organizes the filing system. The manager loves it when everything is neat and tidy.

Management is a talent, just like painting or drawing. Some people have it, most people don't.

The Owner / Entrepreneur / Leader

The entrepreneur is the leader, the visionary! The guy with the big ideas! The Leader sets the mission and pays the managers to bring his vision to life.

The owner operator should know how to wear all these different hats (artist, technician, manager). The owner must use good judgment and find balance between these different mindsets.

The owner must remember that their primary duty is to lead!

It's All About the System

People buy franchise restaurants because they have a proven system to make money. Independent restaurant owners must create their own system to manage their restaurant and make money.

The leader must hire a smart manager and work with them to create a long-term, profitable, self-sustainable system. Most independent restaurant owners fail because they get into business to create sexy food and drink. They think systems are only for places like McDonalds who only hire and train "monkeys". The truth is, most independent restaurant systems are perfectly designed to lose money!

The Operating System

The leader and manager must work together to document every activity that will happen inside the restaurant. This includes things such as the schedule, station check lists and recipes.

Remember, it is the strength of the system and the manager's ability to execute the system that will make or break you! *(Know who has a great restaurant operation system to make money? McDonald's.)*

Smart investors want to buy a system-based business and not a demanding job. Think forward a few years to a time when you might want to sell your restaurant. What is your potential buyer looking for? A profitable business that is cash flowing or a demanding 60 hour a week job, that barely breaks even?

It's your duty to create a system that can be managed & operated by your highly-trained managers & employees. Work ON the Business, not IN it! Here's a good mental exercise for you... Make three assumptions:

1. You are building 10 identical restaurants.
2. You cannot work in any of them.
3. You are building these restaurants to be SOLD in the future.

Maximize Your Working Hours

The Leader and Manager must be on time, stay focused, and get their work done and go home. Remember, you have a family and hopefully a life, so don't be a Martyr.

Set a start and ending time for everything, especially meetings. Keep meetings short, direct, and to the point. Eliminate idle chit-chat and minutia.

Delegate and hold your people accountable for performance. Disorganized people waste an extraordinary amount of time. You and your people must be organized. Everything must have a time and a place. Everything must be in the exact right place at the exact right time.

There are three enemies of success:

1. Coulda
2. Woulda
3. Shoulda

Your job is to stop making excuses for poor performance and design a system that works.

Define the Basic Basics

Like I've mentioned before, the system is the Who, What, Where, When, and exactly How each and every task or function is to be performed.

System = Answers… Things like this:

- Have written recipes with pictures of every menu item.
- Write an effective schedule. Demand 100% attendance from your managers and employees.
- Create exact job checklists for every position (this includes managers, bookkeepers, and your CPA).
- Uniform, Hygiene & Sanitation standards.
- Proper dish washing and cleaning techniques.
- Detailed telephone answering and reservation procedures.
- A complete and detailed script and sales system for waiters and the hostess to follow.

Believe it or not, most independent restaurant owners never take the time to address these important issues. They delegate the responsibility to their managers, who don't understand the process of building a system.

Most managers can never find the time to get the "Important" work done because they are too busy doing the technical work that SHOULD be done by their employees.

Building a business is about creating the concept and designing the system for employees to follow. The goal is to build a system that will do the daily work of the restaurant and liberate the owner/leader to do the work of the entrepreneur which is to:

- Create customers
- Create great products
- Increase sales
- Maximize profits
- Put money in the bank and build wealth
- Enjoy life!

Enforce The System

As the leader, you must build and enforce the system. Your people will never follow your silly little system unless you enforce it. You cannot create the system and then just give it to your managers and employees and expect them to implement it, because they will hide it in a drawer, and nothing will change. You must be 100% committed to building and improving your system. The system is a bright light that shines on every activity in your business so you and your people can see what is really going on.

The sacred cows who work for you will hate the system because the bright light will expose what they have really been up to... which is putting the screws to YOU and your customers!

The next time you find yourself getting upset because someone screwed up, stop and ask yourself, "Did this happen because the employee is stupid or because my system is weak?" Let me save you some time: *Yes,* it is your system. The job of the Leader is to work with management and build an effective system that works.

The Daily Timeline

What happens from the time the first person opens the door in the morning until the door is closed and locked at the end of the night?

I'm talking about everything...

7:45 am – Day Manager Arrival

- Walk exterior and interior of the building, check everything, floor, walls ceiling, equipment – make notes, fix issues.
- Make Coffee – Can't live without coffee.
- Read Manager's Log from previous shift.
- Start working on Day Manager Checklist.

8:00 am – Day Chef Arrival

- Receive and put away deliveries.
- Inspect each kitchen station, food storage, cooler temperature, cleanliness, organization – make notes, fix issues.
- Read Manager's Log from previous shift.
- Check special functions and reservation list.
- Start working on Day Chef Checklist.

9:00 am – Cook #1 & #2 Working: (on time and in uniform)

- Check stations and work areas. Report any issues to Day Chef.
- Start working on their checklists.

10:00 am – Service Staff Working: (on time and in uniform)

- Check stations & work areas. Report any issues to Day Manager.
- Start working on their checklists.

10:45 am –Ready for Lunch Service/Staff Meeting/Inspection:

- Kitchen Inspection
- Dining Room and Public Facilities Inspection.
- Staff Inspection.
- The Stage is set & ready TV's, Music, Lighting, etc.
- Kitchen, bar and side stations 100% ready to go.

This is just a glimpse of what a daily checklist could look like. The point is that these activities happen every day in every restaurant in the world. There are no surprises here. I wonder how many restaurants have a timeline, and how many actually hit the timeline, every day.

The Scientific Method

The greatest invention in history was not the wheel, sliced bread, the iPhone, or the 3D printer. The greatest invention in history was the Scientific Method. The scientific method is the process that allows innovation to happen. The scientific method is the recipe for innovation. Every process in your restaurant must go through some version of the scientific method.

1. Start with a problem or opportunity.
2. Think about how it might be improved, do some research.
3. Make an assumption, guess or hypothesis, of how to improve the procedure or thing.
4. Test the hypothesis by giving it a try.
5. Observe the Results, Analyze Data, Draw Conclusions

When we go through steps 1 – 5, our hypothesis will either work or not. If it does not work the way we hoped, we go back to step #2 and re-think the process.

If it works as we hoped, we celebrate the little victory and then find ways to incorporate the new idea into the system. As time goes on, we find ways to tighten and improve the idea and the system. Successful people use some version of the scientific method in everything they do. This is how innovation is created.

The point is to create a repeatable system to make your business work. The key word is "repeatable".

Your system must be able to be operated by average people with average talent and average brain power. Your success will come from the effectiveness of your system.

- The system as a whole is greater than the "sum of its parts".
- A GOOD system will make average people GOOD.
- A GREAT system will make average people GREAT!
- Your job as the leader is to create a "systems-focused culture".

Be Prepared

I don't know about you, but I'm not talented enough to be unprepared. The system will help you and your people be prepared, poised and ready to Deliver the Customer Promise.

- Proper preparation prevents piss poor performance.
- Failing to plan is planning to fail.

A Business in a Box

Think of your restaurant system as a Business in a Box. The goal of the entrepreneur is to create the restaurant concept, and then work with the managers to build the system to operate the business.

You are not your business. You must stop thinking like a cook or accountant and start thinking like an Entrepreneur & CEO. You must get out of the tasks, and let your people run the daily operation of the business. Your job is to create the system and get out of the way. The job of the leader is to build a business that is "systems dependent" not "owner dependent".

Stop Reinventing the Wheel

There are two very important points here:

1. The smartest business thinkers set the Mission and then work toward the achievement of that mission with constant passion or what is called Constancy of Purpose. Constantly changing the mission is a recipe for disaster.
2. The second point is to quit changing things inside the box, design a smart system and enforce it. Most restaurants fail because they keep changing things and confusing the employees and the customers. Design and set the system and then get out of the way.

The job of the leader happens OUTSIDE the box... OUTSIDE the system. Think of a chain like Chili's. The CEO/Leader does their work at the corporate office. The CEO spends ZERO time working as a cook. On occasion, yes, they will visit a restaurant, but the CEO is busy running the business!

"In the past the man has been first; in the future the system must be first."

- Frederick Taylor, The Father of Scientific Management

Building A System

People buy franchise restaurants because they have a proven system to run the business and make money. Independent restaurant owners must build their own system.

In the beginning:

- The Owner/Leader creates the mission and the vision.
- The Owner/Leader hires the General Manager (GM).
- The Owner/Leader & GM work together to create the Restaurant Concept & The System.
- The General Manager hires the Chef & Service Manager.
- The Chef & Service Manager hire and train their teams to operate within the system and produce the goods and services.
- The goods and services produced lead to delivering the Customer Promise.

Sounds simple because it is. Most restaurant owners think that the Chef and Service Manager know how to build a system and manage a restaurant... the truth is most don't have a clue! Unfortunately, 80% of chefs and managers have the wrong mindset. They are artists or technicians, not managers and leaders.

Great restaurants need leadership and a solid system for doing things. People need a LEADER and a SYSTEM. It is your job to build the system and be a leader!

The Owner Must Manage the Managers

You didn't think they were going to manage themselves, did ya?

In addition to building the system, the main focus of a good Owner/Leader is managing the managers. The Leader must help keep major roadblocks out of the way and hold the manager accountable for the performance of the business.

Hiring the GM is one of the most important decisions the Owner will make regarding the restaurant. Your manager will LITERALLY make or break your business.

Hire a Smart General Manager

Spend serious time interviewing them, have dinner with them, have lunch with them, check their references, visit their previous or current restaurant. Review the training materials from their past job to see if they understand what a system-driven business is.

Once you find a smart General Manager, work with them on these things:

- Build a Business Plan
- Create a solid Operation System
- Create a solid Marketing Plan
- Create an Evaluation System
- Set Measurable Goals
- Get Out of the Way and let the Team Perform
- Measure and Evaluate the Managers Performance vs the Goal
- Work with Management to Improve the System and Performance

Managers Must Believe in the Mission

As the leader you must set clear goals for your manager, and then hold them accountable to accomplish the goals that you have set. Most managers will nod their heads and agree with your vision, and then they will go out and do as they have always done. Every manager must be on the same page as the Owner and strive to accomplish the goal that the Owner has set.

As the Owner/Leader, you must not allow your managers to hoodwink you into believing that your system is stupid. As a good leader, you must replace managers who do not believe in and ignore the system BEFORE they kill the team as well as YOUR business. Remember: They are either for us, or they are against us.

Management 101

Management is figuring out what you want to happen and then building a system to bring that idea, dream or goal to life. This is a matter of biblical importance... there are only two types of managers.

1. Those who are for us.
2. Those who are against us.

There is no middle ground. They are either building and enforcing the system, or they are against you. Your people are either building and improving the system, or they not!

A manager is a coach. I prefer the word coach instead of manager, because everybody has worked for a lousy manager, and the term has a negative connotation for most people. I prefer the word coach because, most of us have had a great coach in our lives who inspired and motivated us to improve and grow.

So, start thinking of yourself, as the Head Coach. Think of your managers as coaches. Are they helping your players improve and learn, or are they fighting against you? Here's an idea: Fire and replace the managers who are against you.

Management is a Talent

Management is a talent that only certain people have. It is much easier to hire a manager to run a business she doesn't understand, than it is to teach a waiter, cook, or bartender to become a manager.

The skill set and interests of a manager are vastly different from the technical skills of a cook, waiter or bartender. That means, just because someone is a good technician, doesn't mean they will become a good manager. Usually, it's just the opposite.

Management can be reduced to seven steps.

1. Determine exactly what you want to happen
2. Create a system to do the work
3. Build a team of winners to perform the work
4. Direct the performance
5. Evaluate the performance
6. Reward success
7. Improve the team and the system (Innovation)

If four employees can make five widgets a day without a manager or system, they should be able to make fifty widgets a day with a good manager directing their performance.

Managers create systems and build teams that allow the process to happen faster, better and more economically. It is the effective management of the system that creates success.

Restaurants have an Owner and three managers:

1. The General Manager (GM)
2. The Chef/Kitchen Manager
3. The Service Manager (FOHM)

Each of these managers must focus on THEIR area of responsibility. They must accomplish their goals with 100% accuracy + 1% for growth. If any of the managers are incompetent and cannot manage their individual areas of responsibility, they must be replaced (quickly) by someone who can accomplish the goals of the department and the business.

Organizational Chart

The Organizational Chart shows the formal Chain of Command, who reports to who and most importantly who is responsible for what. The higher you go in the organization the greater the expectation for performance and professionalism. Therefore, the people at the *front* must conduct themselves as professional managers.

Remember: Better People Build Better Restaurants.

The organizational chart looks like a hierarchical tower on paper; however, it is a "flat" organization that is moving forward toward the goal, every day. The leader is not "on top". They are in the FRONT… leading the team forward toward the goal. It's a parade!

- The Owner/Leader supports the General Manager.
- The General Manager leads and supports the Service Manager & Kitchen Manager.
- The Kitchen Manager supports the Kitchen Staff.
- The Service Manager supports the Service Staff.
- The Entire Team supports each other.

The goal is to deliver the Customer Promise. Every person in the organization must do their job 100% + 1% for growth, every day.

Manager Checklists

I am about to give you a list of duties for the three key managers in your business. Your natural tendency is to skim the list and move on, BUT that is not what I want you to do. I want you to print off the lists and compare them to the checklist or job description that your people have.

If your list is better than my list, then good for you. If my list is better than your list, I want you to go over it with your people and see if it can help everybody improve. The second thing you can do with my silly little list is, rate your people with it. Give them a 1 – 5 score on every single item on the list. Doesn't that sound fun! Honestly, the idea of you doing this thrills me beyond words. So, be sure to do it. What could be more important than managing your managers and helping them grow?

The General Manager

The GM directs and manages the system. The GM manages:

1. The Business & Finances
2. Team Building & HR
3. The Physical Building
4. Kitchen Manager/Chef
5. The Service Manager (FOHM)

Business & Finances:

- The Annual Budget
- Sales vs Goal (10% annual sales increase)
- The 30-30-30-10
- Cost of Goods (Food & Bar)
- Labor Cost
- Other Cost
- The Bottom Line – Profit

- Sales Taxes – Paid on Time!
- Accounts Payable & Receivable
- Payroll & Payroll Taxes – Paid on Time!
- Profit Distribution Paid to the Owner – Paid on Time!

Team Building & HR:

- Employee related paperwork
- Networking & Recruiting the next generation of great players
- Building future managers with the "Stair-Step Training System"

The Physical Building:

- Preventive maintenance and cleaning.
- Licenses, permits, and inspections.

Also, the GM is the leader of the Marketing Team. They also drive innovation. The GM is responsible to improve and tighten the system on a daily basis. They find future business & growth opportunities and work with the community outside the restaurant.

In short, the GM is responsible for EVERYTHING that happens in the restaurant, good or bad.

The Kitchen Manager/Chef

The job of the kitchen manager/chef is to lead and manage the kitchen, the production. The Chefs main objectives are to:

1. Deliver the Customer Promise (internal customers, waiters).
2. Increase Sales with Amazing Food
3. Keep the kitchen perfectly organized.
4. Build a winning kitchen team.
5. Train & manage the staff.
6. Meet financial goals.

Deliver the Customer Promise:

- Produce high quality goods to exact specifications.
- Produce all products to recipe, quality & presentation standards.
- Purchase groceries to the highest quality specification.
- Maintain proper food storage and handling.

Keep the kitchen perfectly organized:

- Every station must be set up on time, as per diagram.
- Every piece of equipment must be in proper working order.
- Floor, walls and ceiling must be clean.
- Maintain surgical sanitation and cleanliness standards.
- Kitchen must be closed properly at end of shift.

Build a winning team in the kitchen:

- Network & recruit great players.
- Train the kitchen staff.
- Write an effective schedule.
- Demand 100% attendance.
- Insist on professional uniforms, knives and hand tools.

Train & Manage the Staff:

- Create Opening/During/Closing checklists for all positions.
- Monitor completion of checklists.
- Create & administer tests – operation, sanitation, food, financial.
- Evaluate staff/60-second evaluations/Quarterly evaluations.
- Operate the stair step training system

Meet Financial Goals:

- Manage the par purchase system.
- Get the highest yield possible from every product.
- Keep food and supply inventory at par / Reduce waste to zero.
- Maximize the profits of the restaurant.
- Manage Costs within budgeted Guidelines.
- Maximize profit for the business.

The Service Manager

Manages the Bar and the Dining Room. The Service Manager's goals are:

1. Deliver the Customer Promise
2. Build a winning service team
3. Build a great service system
4. Increase Sales by at Least 10% Every Year
5. Improve Financial Performance

Deliver the Customer Promise:

- Orchestrate the Customer Experience.
- Create Wow Experiences for each and every guest we serve.
- Build the Restaurant Club.
- Manage the reservation system.
- Manage the telephone answering system.
- Keep the public areas clean, organized, and well maintained.

Build a Winning Team:

- Train and manage the sales and service team.
- Write an effective schedule – Demand 100% attendance.
- Manage the bar to the same standards as the kitchen.

- Create and administer tests – operation, sanitation, service, wine, bar, food.
- Evaluate the sales & Service Staff.
- Measure, Rank, Post the Results.
- Reward the Best Ranked Waiters with Best Stations.
- Manage the Stair Step Training System.

Build the Service System:

- Create station operational standards.
- Steps of Service Guidelines.
- Create Scripts for the Waiters to follow.
- Create opening – during and closing checklists for all positions.
- Monitor completion of checklists.
- Every station set up on time as per diagram.
- Equipment must be clean and in proper working order.
- Sanitation & cleanliness standards for employees & equipment.
- Floor, walls, ceiling, windows and doors will be clean and freshly painted.
- FOH will be closed properly at end of shift – set for the next day.
- Constantly Tighten & Improve the training system.

Financial Goals:

- Beat last year sales by a minimum of 10% (no excuses)
- Manage Costs within budgeted Guidelines.
- Maximize profit for the business.

Managers are Measured by Performance

Managers are measured by the team's ability to deliver the Customer Promise and achieve financial results. (no excuses)

We measure:

- Top Line Sales vs the Goal
- Food Cost vs the Goal
- Beverage Cost vs the Goal
- Labor Cost vs the Goal
- Other Costs vs the Goal
- Bottom Line Profit vs the Goal

Managers Must Face Reality

Face the facts, admit the problems, and don't sweep them under the rug. Work to solve the problems. Never play the blame game, it's a huge waste of time. Solving problems is what we do. Don't bitch about the problem or the person that screwed up... Fix it!

Problems present opportunities to improve the system. When a problem happens, you must fix the system by creating and documenting a new procedure for your people to follow. Teach them how to do it the "right way", so the problem doesn't happen again. This is not politics, this is your business, and your people depend on you.

"Honesty is the first chapter in the book of wisdom."

- Thomas Jefferson

If You Can't Clean, You Can't Work Here!

If your restaurant is struggling, chances are that your restaurant is dirty and in need of a good scrub! This is a great way to get your people involved and moving. A dirty restaurant says, "We don't care."

Start by Making a list of every task that needs to be done, and delegate the tasks. This will let you know immediately who is, and who isn't on your side. Think Pac Man.

Cleaning your restaurant is the first step in the transformation. Clean everything. The floor, walls, ceiling, equipment, top to bottom. If you need help making a cleaning list, call the health inspector, they will be thrilled that you called and glad to help! *They really would.*

Get rid of everything that you don't need. Every restaurant has junk lying around. Tools and stuff that stopped working long ago. Either fix it, sell it, or throw it out. Make room for the important stuff you actually need.

Fix or replace all broken equipment. Your people can't work with broken equipment. Every piece of equipment must be in good working order. Move the furniture and equipment around. Move stuff around to improve flow and efficiency. This will also create a new vibe, and let people know that something new and exciting is happening.

"If you have time to lean, you have time to clean."

- Ray Kroc, founder of McDonalds

168

Treat the Cause... Not the Effect

The symptom of a hangover is a headache and an upset stomach, these symptoms can be relieved by aspirin and ice cream, or Angostura bitters and club soda. But a hangover can be AVOIDED by not over-indulging to begin with.

A high food cost is the symptom of bad management. A late or missed shift is the result of a bad employee, a lousy schedule and a weak manager. It is much smarter to AVOID problems, than waste time trying to fix them. Ignorance is no excuse.

Fix the System

Before you start screaming and yelling at some kid who screwed up, it is best to check to see if the error is the fault of the system or the manager. I have learned to find out exactly what the problem is by tracing it all the way back to the root cause. This way I know who to scream at, before I start to yell. Most of the time, the problem was caused by a weakness in the system or a bad manager. *Sometimes, I yell at myself!* Most of your employees want to do a good job. It's up to us to give them the answers, so they can perform and win!

Focus on the possible, not the "what if" or "the impossible". Don't allow people to waste your time with trivial matters. Delegate and teach your staff to handle the important details that happen every day. Then, get out of the way and let them do their job.

Finish

You must have a strong finish after every shift. Imagine, Michael Phelps swimming to the finish line! The entire restaurant must be clean, organized and ready for the next shift.

All food must be properly protected and stored. Everything must have a place, and everything must be in its place. Don't allow your staff to be sloppy and doddle at the finish line!

The world rates ability in men by what they *finish*, not by what they attempt. Success is not optional. You are here to achieve the goal. Anything short of the goal is failure. Remember that failure is a temporary condition, not a destination. When you fail, get your ass back up and take a bigger swing!

A House of Cards

A restaurant is like a house of cards, if you pull the wrong card, the entire house will topple. A restaurant is a very intricate framework, with thousands of interdependent parts. It takes years to build a successful restaurant, and only a matter of weeks, days, or even minutes, to destroy one. The smartest way to keep your house of cards from falling down is to glue it together with Super Glue– Your system is the glue that holds everything together!

Your restaurant is made up of several key components:

- Brand, reputation, location
- Food and beverage style, quality, service and cleanliness
- The physical building, furniture, and equipment
- Intellectual property, recipes, operating systems and knowledge
- Your Customers, Employees and Managers

The common denominator in most of the above examples is PEOPLE. The restaurant business is labor intensive and people-driven. The success or failure of your business will always come down to the quality of the people on your team.

Losing a critical employee or manager at the wrong time can be disastrous. Hiring and keeping a bad employee can be even worse.

The right people will make it possible for you to accomplish your goals. The wrong people will drive you crazy! Of all the things on your "To Do List", hiring, training, and managing your people, must be Number One.

People will come and go. You must work to build a system that will hold it all together. The System is the glue that holds the people and procedures together. The system will need to adapt to changing conditions.

Your business provides the cash that makes your life work, it is your duty to protect the business and the restaurant, no matter what. Every decision that you make must take into consideration:

- The satisfaction of the customer
- The success of your people
- The short- and long-term wellness of the business

Pulling the wrong card at the wrong time and allowing the restaurant to come tumbling down is never in the best interest of the business. For every action, there will be an equal and opposite reaction. Think before you act.

Chapter Recap

The key concepts in this chapter are:

- The System is The Who, What, Where, When and Why of Your Restaurant
- There are Three Ways to do Everything – Do It The RIGHT Way – The First Time
- Eliminate Grunge – Simplicity is the Ultimate Sophistication
- Two Ways to Train – Tribal Method and The Written Manual
- Work ON the business – not IN it.
- Maximize Your Working Hours – Become a Modern-Day Frederick Taylor
- Use the Scientific Method to Innovate and Solve Problems
- Stop Reinventing the Wheel – Stick with the Mission – Constancy of Purpose.
- You Need an Organizational Chart – You are not Google.
- Restaurants Have Three Managers – The GM, Kitchen Manager, Service Manager.
- The Leader Must Manage the Managers – They are NOT going to Manage Themselves.
- Have the Guts to Be Honest with Yourself and Face Reality
- Your Restaurant is a House of Cards – The System is the Glue That Holds It Together.

While the ideas in this chapter are still fresh in your mind. I want you to make a list of 10 THINGS that you can do to improve your system.

Fundamental #8:
Innovate, Improve & Adapt

Could you imagine telling Auguste Escoffier, Thomas Edison, Steve Jobs, Warren Buffett, or Elon Musk that your restaurant is running at peak efficiency and there isn't a single thing that could be improved? I can't either. We all have room to improve.

Your level of "acceptance" will determine your "level of greatness". What you *do*, defines who you are. This is true in your work, at home, and in your spiritual life:

- Little people do little things.
- Average people do average things.
- Great people do *great* things.

"There's a better way to do it. Find it."

> - Thomas A. Edison

Organize Your Thoughts

The process we are about to go through will require you to think deeply. This will help you get focused on the most important things.

This is where your future innovation and "aha moments" will come from.

At the end of each fundamental, I asked you to make a list of 10 things that you could do to improve your performance in that area. You should now have 70 golden ideas that can move you to the next level.

1. 10 things you can do to achieve your mission
2. 10 things you can do to improve yourself
3. 10 things you can do to improve your team.
4. 10 ways to improve the customer experience.
5. 10 ways to increase sales.
6. 10 ways to manage your money smarter.
7. 10 ways to improve your operating system.

I also asked you to write the mission of your restaurant. First, be sure to save your lists. They will be helpful down the road and fun to look back at in a few years, when you are living the Good Life.

Now I want you to go back and look at your ideas from each of the seven chapters and write down the top two ideas for improving each fundamental. For example:

- Improve Myself #1:
- Improve Myself #2:
- Achieve the Mission #1:
- Achieve the Mission #2:
- Improve the Team #1:
- Improve the Team #2:
- … and so on

The Vital Few

Take a deep look at the list you wrote down and ask yourself which THREE are the most vital? Then rewrite them down in order.

For example:

1. Vital Idea #1
2. Vital Idea #2
3. Vital Idea #3

Now look at the vital few, which ONE THING is the most important? Which ONE of the ideas above will move your restaurant forward toward the ultimate goal?

Which ONE THING will make life better for the customer, the team members and the owner? What is the ONE THING that you can do today (right now) that will move you toward your ultimate goal and achievement of your mission?

When you determine what your ONE THING is, write it down again:

- My ONE THING is:

Now you know what the most important "One Thing" thing is, ask yourself these questions:

- What is the best way to do this ONE THING?
- How can I do this ONE THING better, faster, smarter?

Imagine what could happen if everybody on your team, used this same simple process to figure out what their ONE THING is.

I recommend that you have your chef, bartender, service manager and general manager read this book and answer these questions. This simple process will revolutionize your restaurant in the next 90-Days. The journey of a thousand miles begins with one single step. Don't take too much on too fast:

- One thing done = Money
- Five things NOT done, or HALF done = No money

The 80/20 Principle

The 80/20 Principle states that 80% of your efforts lead to 20% of your positive results, and 20% of your efforts lead to 80% of your positive results. This is also called the Pareto Principle. This is a very popular management concept today, because it is *brilliant*. So, be sure to use it to your advantage.

Vilfredo Pareto was an Italian economist who wrote in 1896, that 80% of the land and wealth in Italy was controlled by 20% of the people. Pareto further determined, that this same breakdown applied to a number of other countries abroad. Today the Pareto Principle is also called The 80/20 Rule, or sometimes "The Law of the Vital Few".

Here's an example of how the 80/20 Principle works:

- Imagine a group of 100 people with $1,000,000 of wealth.
- The Top 20 people would have $40,000 each…
  (80% of the wealth, or $800,000, divided by 20)
- The Bottom 80 people would have $2,500 each…
  (20% of the wealth or $200,000, divided by 80)

When we apply the Pareto Principle to the Top 20% of the people who share $800,000:

- We find that the Top 20% of that group (4 people) have $160,000 each… *(80% of that wealth, or $640,000, divided by 4.)*
- The Remaining 80% (16 people) have $10,000 each… *(20% of that wealth, $160,000, divided by 16)*

Here's what the new spread between the 100 people looks like:

- 4 People have $160,000 each
- 16 People have $10,000 each
- 80 People have $2,500 each...
  (this group also has an 80/20, by the way)

This is how the world still works today. In fact, this is how the world has and will always work. There are the haves and the have nots. The "doers" and the "don't-ers". Equal distribution does not exist.

Here's what the 80/20 Theory means to you:

- 20% of your customers create 80% of your current & future sales.
- 20% of your staff create 80% of the positive results.
- 80% of your staff are only creating 20% of the positive results.
- 20% of your employees are creating 80% of your problems.
- 20% of your menu items create 80% of your current sales
- 80% of your menu items only create 20% of your sales.
- 20% of your menu items are making your customers return.
- 80% of your menu items might be chasing people away.
- 80% of your personal effort is only creating 20% of your success.
- 20% of your efforts are creating 80% of your success.

If 80% of your efforts lead to 20% of your success, and 20% of your efforts lead to 80% of your success, then you should spend all your time on the vital 20% that produces the best results, and delegate the rest.

Smart Time Management

If you really want to improve your time management and effectiveness, picking the right project and working on the right things is the smart way to go. Inversely, spending weeks and months on the wrong thing will lead to nothing. Smart leaders get their teams focused on "the vital few" things that move the ball forward.

Spend Time on Important Matters

Spend time on important matters. *I love that phrase*. It's very powerful. This lesson is about what project to work on first. The important things, the right things. Wasting time on the wrong things is an expensive waste of time and resources. Great leaders get the right things done.

President Dwight D. Eisenhower said that there are two types of tasks:

1. Urgent tasks
2. Important tasks

Important tasks are strategic items that move us forward, such as planning and training. Urgent tasks are items that demand immediate attention. Eisenhower divided tasks into four different groups:

1. Important & Urgent
2. Important, but not Urgent
3. Urgent, but not Important
4. Not Urgent or Important

The Time Matrix

Management coach Steven Covey took the Eisenhower principle a step further and turned it into a Time Matrix which shows the relationship between Important and Urgent items. I am going to blend these two concepts together and relate them to your restaurant.

The best management technique is to "work on the most important things first". As simple as that may appear, this can be very difficult because when you're in the middle of it, everything seems important. The trick is to stop and differentiate between Important and Urgent matters.

An Important item will make an impact on the business over the short and long term. Important items include setting goals, creating a business plan, a marketing plan, and a financial plan to achieve a ten percent profit. Important items are financial and operational things related to the system.

Think of them as things that are done at the corporate office of a chain restaurant, outside the system. These items include job checklists, documenting food and bar recipes, costing and pricing the menus, and setting service and cleaning standards.

Important items are related to the creation of your Core Concept and system. They will move you closer to delivering the Customer Promise.

An Urgent item is a task that demands immediate attention and occurs over and over, such as writing the schedule, answering the phone, taking a reservation, doing the food order, running food, seating guests, and covering shifts for people who didn't show up for work.

These things must be performed inside the system by the managers and staff. Understanding the difference between Important and Urgent tasks will help you move from firefighter to an effective leader. Leaders accomplish Important tasks, and they give their people the answers.

The following quotes are very appropriate today, though they were written hundreds of years ago. Some things never change.

"Time is what we want most, but what we use worst."

    - William Penn

"Better three hours too soon than one minute late."

    - William Shakespeare

"It's not enough to be busy, so are the ants. The question is: What are we busy about?"

    - Henry David Thoreau

Quad #1: Important & Urgent Tasks

This is the Action Quad. It represents the urgent and important things that happen during the daily operation of your restaurant. This includes answering the phone, seating customers, producing food and drinks, running food and turning tables. This is where real work gets done, this is where your true customer satisfaction comes from. You must train your shift managers and team members to do this work.

When you (the leader) spend all your time in Quad #1, (doing routine work) you will never have time for your real job of leadership, management and planning. Spending too much time in Quad #1, will lead to stress, frustration and anger. When the leader is doing the routine work, who is driving the bus?

Quad #2: Important but Not Urgent Tasks

This is the Executive & Leadership Quad. This is where you must spend 80% - 100% of your time. These are things such as planning, marketing, budgeting, team building, coaching and training. This quad is about building the system, recruiting and training your people to operate smoothly and profitably without you. *That is what a leader is supposed to do! Do not to confuse HARD WORK with RESULTS.*

The leader must focus on completing the IMPORTANT items in Quad #2, so the staff can have the information (the answers) they need to do their job in quad #1. Focusing on the completion of Important Quad #2 tasks will eliminate most of your problems and the need for crisis management.

The goal is to build the system and train your people to execute the IMPORTANT/URGENT tasks that happen over and over, day after day.

Although leadership and planning items are very important, they often get shoved aside, because most managers and owners get sucked into the urgent trap of quad #1, or quad #3. Spending too much time in Quad #1 and #3 is actually a sign of laziness, and a lack of discipline

Quad #2 also includes taking care of yourself. This means getting some exercise, eating right and taking time off to revitalize yourself. This quad also includes reading and learning new skills. Try taking a walk and listening to a podcast, it will change your life.

As a restaurant owner and operator, I try to find a balance between Important tasks and Urgent tasks. I realize that there are days when I must put my head down and work in the operation, and there are other days when I can focus on planning and leadership activities.

The next two Quads are "Below the Line Activities" that must be minimized or avoided.

Quad #3: Urgent, but Not Important Tasks

This is the Waste Quad. These activities must be minimized. The biggest time waster that you own is your smart phone, that's right, about 80% of the stuff you do with your phone is either a total waste or a distraction that takes you away from getting important work done. The #1 problem with your phone is that it constantly interrupts your train of thought. If you really want to get IMPORTANT things done, you need to turn your phone off for set periods of the day. I know you have a million reasons why that would be bad, but just try it.

Imagine going out on a date with your husband or wife without your phone? Wow! Liberating!

Then, there are things like, TV, Facebook, Twitter, Fantasy Football and video games. There are also things that pop up, like the electricity going out or the cooler going down. These things kill our productivity and don't help us move the ball forward.

Quad #3 activities also happen when your personal life spills into your work life, with things like interruptions from friends and co-workers who just stop by to chit-chat —calls from bill collectors, visits from the police department, or that psycho ex-girlfriend or ex-boyfriend who just stopped by to ruin your life.

Quad #3 Tasks also include times when we say yes to people or projects that we should have delegated or said NO to in the first place. Spending too much time in Quad #3, will lead to worry, guilt and loss of focus. When you spend all your time in Quad #1 & Quad #3 your life will be full of stress. *Sound Familiar?*

Quad #4: Not Urgent or Important Tasks

This is the Self-Destructive Quad. These activities must be avoided. They include things like smoking cigarettes, smoking pot, excessive drinking, using illegal drugs and whoring about.

Quad #4 also includes negative thinking, bitching, complaining and gossip that will tear your restaurant apart.

Spending too much time in Quad #4 will lead to loss of health, mental burnout and the death of your restaurant. If you really want to win, stay out of Quad #4. *Really!*

Smart Quad Management

As the leader you must focus on & complete 100% of the Quad #2 duties BEFORE you spend one minute on Quad #1 things. This is very difficult to do, because of the temptation of the fun work in Quad #1.

Remember this; Lazy un-disciplined people allow Quad #1 activities to pull them away from their real job of LEADING and PLANNING. They do this because Quad #2 activities require them to think and *thinking is the hardest work there is.*

As the leader you must create the system and design the tools for your managers and staff to use. Then, you must train your shift managers and staff to USE THE TOOLS and focus on the Important & Urgent items in Quad #1. If you really want to win, you must minimize Quad #3 and avoid Quad #4.

FOOD GURU TIME MATRIX		
	URGENT	**NOT URGENT**
IMPORTANT	**Operational Activities** Answer the Phone Seat Customers Produce Food & Drinks Run Food Turn Tables **Effect** Achievement / Success Stress / Anxiety / Exhaustion	**Leadership Activities** Planning Team Building Management Coaching Financial Planning Marketing **Effect** Happiness / Winning Satisfaction / Life Balance
	URGENT	**NOT URGENT**
NOT IMPORTANT	**Personal Activities** Smoke Breaks Fantasy Football Texting / Facebook Covering Missed Shifts Bad Personal Relationships **Effect** Frustration / Anger Negative Attitude / Burnout	**Wasteful Activities** Excess TV Excessive Drinking Smoking Ganja Gambling "Whore-ing" **Effect** Boredom / Detachment Loss of Control

It's Time for Action

We all know what needs to be done. The problem is setting the priorities and then actually doing it. Think about this:

- How many diets does it take to lose weight? *The ONE that works!*
- How many people know that smoking cigarettes is bad for their health? *Yet, how many people still smoke?*
- How many people know that exercise is good for their health? *And still, how many people actually exercise on a regular basis?*

Most people know what to do; they just don't *do* it! Why? Because it involves change, and change is hard!

Focus On The Simple "Above The Line Activities"

Remember, simple above the line activities are easy to do—and easy not to do. Simple actions done consistently over time will compound off each other, and before you know it, you will have a great business.

These Eight Basic Fundamentals can be used to create a simple, black & white system with very little "grey area" or grunge.

The good and the bad thing about a simple system is that there is nowhere to hide. Everyone in the organization must perform to the standards of the company and the system. Everyone must lead, follow, or get out of the way, and by the way, this includes YOU!

It's like Les Brown says, *"If you do what is easy, your life will be hard. If you do what is hard, your life will be easy."*

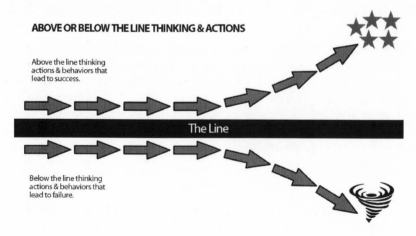

ABOVE OR BELOW THE LINE THINKING & ACTIONS

Above the line thinking actions & behaviors that lead to success.

The Line

Below the line thinking actions & behaviors that lead to failure.

What's Important Now (W.I.N.)

Every restaurant manager and chef has daily operational responsibility: The restaurant must produce the goods and services. In addition to your own urgent operational responsibilities, you have important projects that need to be completed.

In this chapter we have just taken 70 ideas (hopefully you did this) and reduced them down to the "Most Important 14", which in case you were wondering, just so happens to be the Top 20%. Then you reduced the Top 20% down to just three, The Vital Few. Then out of those three vital few, you determined what your most important ONE THING was.

Here's how to drastically improve your restaurant.

1. Go to work on #1, and don't stop until it is complete.
2. Then work on #2 until it is complete.
3. Then work on and complete #3.

When you have completed these three vital things, then you can zoom out and look at your restaurant from a distance and ask yourself "How have these vital things changed the landscape?"

The Vital Three

I have found that when we accomplish the three most vital things on our "to-do" list, it has a dramatic effect, and often changes the importance and priority of remaining list. Sometimes the accomplishment of our Vital Three, can make our entire list irrelevant... here's why:

Accomplishing the vital few things every day will move you way above the clouds; it will change your entire perspective and paradigm. You will begin to see things you have never seen before. Your entire belief system and priorities will shift.

Once you have completed your vital few, I want you to re-read this book and make new lists for each of the fundamentals. Then, you can compare both lists and go to work on your new Vital Few. I guarantee, this process will help you get and stay focused on the most important projects. I wholeheartedly believe if you continue this process for long enough, your restaurant will become one of the best restaurants in your market, and just maybe, the world.

STOP!

I want you to think about that comment "World's Best" for a minute. Do you believe that you have the potential to be the "World's Best" at anything? I challenge you to start thinking like one of the best in the world. You can do this by asking better questions.

"What is the BEST way to do this?"

181

This simple little question can--and will--change your life. All you have to do is ask the question and then do the work, take the action. Stop selling yourself short; You Can Do It! Don't be afraid to do your best. Don't be afraid to put yourself out there.

Imagine what could happen if the Owner, the GM, the Chef, and the Service Manager of your restaurant all do the same thing. In fact, I believe all your key people should participate in this process. It is the best and fastest way to transform your business. Imagine what you can accomplish in the next 90-days, when you get serious and focus on the right projects.

I'll tell you what will happen: Your restaurant will improve by leaps and bounds! You may never become the World's Best restaurant, but you will get into the Top 5%. Think about that: Moving from where you are today to the TOP 5% will change your life.

Great leaders constantly update their "to-do" lists and follow-through to insure everyone is always focused on—and accomplishing—the *right* things.

Every Manager and Employee must have written goals with reasonable time limits. You must go through this exercise with your key people to insure they are working on and accomplishing the RIGHT things!

Over the Rainbow

What would you attempt to do if you knew you could not fail? Leap and the net will appear!

The Power of 1% Improvements

The information in this book will catapult your knowledge-base into the Top 5% of all restaurant owners. You don't need an MBA from Harvard. All you have to do is take action and commit to doing your job 100%, plus a simple 1%, every single day for the rest of your life.

If you can do that, your life will see an exponential shift. Before long, you will be living the life of your dreams.

Now is the time for action. It's time to stop talking and start doing! When you combine the information in this book with 1% more action and focus, a miracle will happen!

Here is fun concept that will help your thinking:

- At 211-degrees' water is hot.
- At 212-degrees' water begins to boil.
- Boiling water creates steam.
- Steam can power a locomotive!

Think of how one degree of heat changes everything! Imagine what 1% more action and focus could do for you and your business! I challenge you to commit to doing your job 100% and making a 1% improvement—every day for the rest of your life!

This is your life. This is not a dress rehearsal!

Mental Resistance

When you start to explain these ideas to your friends, family, partners, managers, and employees, they will most likely have doubts about your new vision and your sanity. Your new ideas will most likely scare them to their core. They may think you have gone mad. They will probably try their best to talk you out of moving forward with your crazy new plan. Change is very scary to most people.

If you are convincing and strong enough to get past the fears and doubts of your family, partners and managers, you will only have one major obstacle left. In the middle of the night, you will be awakened by the strongest negative force in the universe: Mental Resistance.

This mental resistance will provide you with every reason why your new plan will fail. Mental Resistance will tell you exactly how your ideas are too good to be true. The worst part of this mental resistance is... the resistance will be coming from INSIDE YOUR MIND!

The strongest enemy you will ever encounter is your own mental resistance to success:

- Mental Resistance wants you to stay where you are today.
- Mental Resistance wants to keep you in the bind you are in.
- Mental Resistance does not want you to succeed.
- Mental Resistance is your mortal enemy; it is your Goliath.

You cannot negotiate or reason with this mental monster. It will never give you a break. It will hound you until you abandon your true goals and dreams. The only way to defeat this mental monster is to KILL IT!

Once you kill your mental monster, the universe will begin to work with you to create a brand-new world where you will accomplish your goals and realize your dreams. The universe can and will help you create the life you've always wanted. This is the fight of your life. But first you must believe. Leap and the net will appear.

Chapter Recap

The key concepts in this chapter are:

- Organize Your Thoughts
- Determine Your Vital Few
- Work On the Most IMPORTANT Thing First
- Use the 80/20 Principle
- The Best Time Managers – Spend Time on Important Matters
- Use the Time Matrix to Your Advantage: Avoid Quad 3 & 4
- Use the Scientific Method to Solve Problems and Innovate
- Work on the Vital Few to Achieve Greatness
- Use the Power of 1% Improvement.
- The Best Way to Beat Mental Resistance is to KILL IT!

The 9 Dot Puzzle Answer

As you remember, I put this puzzle in the Owner Mindset Chapter for you to solve, and instead of putting the answer on the next page, I hid it back here. Hopefully, you solved the 9 dot puzzle by yourself, if you didn't that doesn't mean you are stupid, it just means you're about average or that you are impatient and you gave up and came here for the answer.

Either way, here's a quick refresher. The 9 dot puzzle has been around for centuries, it goes all the way back to the Egyptians, who used ladybugs in the desert sand to create the 9 dots. It is an awesome brain teaser. It is considered by many people smarter than me to be the origin of outside-the-box thinking exercise. The objective is:

- Connect all nine dots below
- Using a pen or pencil
- With only four straight lines
- You cannot lift the pen from the paper

Yes, this problem is solvable! Please spend some time thinking about it before you give up and go find the answer. This is a great test in *self-reliance*. You have the power inside your brain to solve it. This problem involves creative, outside-the-box thinking. You will have to let go of your preconceived ideas and open your mind to new possibilities. You will have to step back and see the big picture.

This puzzle requires abstract thinking, as do many of your biggest problems. Here's how that works in this situation. Most people see the 9 Dot Puzzle as a box, defined by the outer dots. They try to solve the problem literally "inside the box", but this requires outside-the-box thinking.

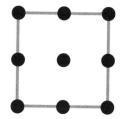

They try to stay within the framework created by the dots. Big thinkers have the ability to step back and see the problem as a whole, they think outside the box. When you think *outside* the box, you realize that you can use the entire piece of paper to solve the problem, you are not limited to the space within the box, or inside the dots. Ok, so turn the page and see the answer.

The Answer

If you haven't seen this before, or you didn't solve it, I'll bet this is a real mind blower! I love it! This really defines outside-the-box thinking. I didn't figure this puzzle out on my own. I looked at it for about 5 minutes, then I turned the page to see the answer, the suspense was killing me.

The coolest thing is that even though, I took the lazy way out, the solution still blew my mind. Once I saw it, the solution was so obvious, I felt like a moron. It had not yet occurred to me, to draw the lines outside the dots. My mind had me limited by the outer dots.

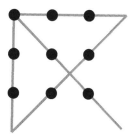

My first reaction was "WOW! This really is outside-the-box thinking at its finest." My second thought was, "Why didn't I just sit back and give this some time to work out?" The simple answer is that I'm way too impatient. The harder answer is that I really didn't want to work that hard, I was on vacation, reading a book on an airplane.

All the people (who haven't seen this before) have the same reaction. They look at it for about ten seconds, then they look at me for the answer. Then, they look back at the puzzle again, then back at me. This is because at first, the problem looks very difficult, then, after some reflection, the problem shifts in their mind from difficult to impossible.

I can imagine a Great Sensei Master giving this puzzle to a student and letting him sweat it out for about five years, until he either became enlightened and solved it, or went insane by the torment of an impossible task.

The solution to the 9 Dot Puzzle is a great metaphor for the problems that you and I face every single day in our restaurants. We must learn to open our minds and look for solutions outside our limits and comfort zones. We must learn to relax, be calm, take our time, reflect, and look beyond the problem because the solution is always outside our current paradigm, outside the limited scope of the dots and the box... our box.

Being an impatient American, who is always in a hurry to check everything off of our to do list is one of our greatest weaknesses. The speed, that the world is moving at today, has made it almost impossible for us to stop and use our brilliant minds to contemplate and think deeply about what is going on around us.

I hope that this fun little exercise with the 9 Dot puzzle helps you realize that there are many things, within the power of your mind. You need to stop the insanity and think. Give yourself time to reflect on what you can do with the amazing and abundant resources that are all around you.

The other lesson that the 9 Dot Puzzle teaches us, is while we may not have the answers ourselves, there is always someone who has already solved the exact same problem. Someone who knows that the impossible, is actually pretty simple once you figure it out.

Conclusion

Most restaurant owners and managers wear themselves out chasing thousands of small Urgent details that keep them trapped inside their cage. Because of this we don't have the time or mental energy to focus on the Important things that lead to the target.

My goal is to help you build the restaurant of your dreams and have a better life. My goal is to help you focus on the Important things, the Eight Basic Fundamentals that lead directly to the target.

The Eight Basic Fundamentals are:

1. Set & Achieve a Noble Goal
2. Develop the Owner Mindset
3. Build a Winning Team
4. Build a Customer-Centered Brand
5. Build a Better Marketing & Sales System
6. Build a Better Money Management System
7. Build a Better Operating System
8. Improve, Innovate & Adapt

These Eight Basic Fundamentals can save you a decade of trial and error, if you use them. These Eight Basic Fundamentals are the foundation of every great restaurant. You will be amazed with the transformation that can happen in your restaurant and your life as you put them to work.

I hope you learned something that will help you improve your restaurant and your life. If you have any questions or comments, I would love to hear them, just send me an email at foodguru@foodguru.com.

I also have two ways great to help you improve:

1. The Food Guru's Build a Better Restaurant Podcast & Weekly Pep Talk. You can find it on your favorite podcast channel by searching "Build a Better Restaurant".
2. One-on-One coaching. Just send me a message if you are interested, and we can both roll up our sleeves and kick some ass together.

I wish you all the best,
Chef Peter Harman, The Food Guru

Training
Why work for BSB

Values
   - Employee
   - customer exp. - value of transaction
        \$ = work, labor, talent, ability

restaurant = FT career
Clean & finish

Made in the USA
Middletown, DE
19 August 2019